Other titles in the
A Retreat With... *Series:*

A RETREAT WITH MARK

A RETREAT WITH MARK

Embracing Discipleship

Stephen C. Doyle, O.F.M.

ST. ANTHONY MESSENGER PRESS

Cincinnati, Ohio

Cover illustration by Steve Erspamer, S.M.
Cover and book design by Mary Alfieri
Electronic format and pagination by Sandy L. Digman

ISBN 0-86716-324-0

Published by St. Anthony Messenger Press
Printed in the U.S.A.

DEDICATION

Kevin Mullen, O.F.M.
Gordon Murphy, O.F.M.
Hugh Hines, O.F.M.
Kevin Kriso, O.F.M.
Bob Martin

"I alone can do it, but I cannot do it alone."

Thank you

Contents

Introducing A Retreat With...

Twenty years ago I made a weekend retreat at a
Franciscan house on the coast of New Hampshire. The
retreat director's opening talk was as lively as a long-
range weather forecast. He told us how completely God
loves each one of us—without benefit of lively anecdotes
or fresh insights.

As the friar rambled on, my inner critic kept up a
sotto voce commentary: "I've heard all this before." "Wish
he'd say something new that I could chew on." "That poor
man really doesn't have much to say." Ever hungry for
manna yet untasted, I devalued any experience of hearing
the same old thing.

After a good night's sleep, I awoke feeling as peaceful
as a traveler who has at last arrived safely home. I walked
across the room toward the closet. On the way I passed
the sink with its small framed mirror on the wall above.
Something caught my eye like an unexpected presence. I
turned, saw the reflection in the mirror and said aloud,
"No wonder he loves me!"

This involuntary affirmation stunned me. What or
whom had I seen in the mirror? When I looked again, it
was "just me," an ordinary person with a lower-than-
average reservoir of self-esteem. But I knew that in the
initial vision I had seen God-in-me breaking through like a
sudden sunrise.

At that moment I knew what it meant to be made in
the divine image. I understood right down to my size

1

eleven feet what it meant to be loved exactly as I was. Only later did I connect this revelation with one granted to the Trappist monk-writer Thomas Merton. As he reports in *Conjectures of a Guilty Bystander*, while standing all unsuspecting on a street corner one day, he was overwhelmed by the "joy of being...a member of a race in which God Himself became incarnate.... There is no way of telling people that they are all walking around shining like the sun."

As an absentminded homemaker may leave a wedding ring on the kitchen windowsill, so I have often mislaid this precious conviction. But I have never forgotten that particular retreat. It persuaded me that the Spirit rushes in where it will. Not even a boring director or a judgmental retreatant can withstand the "violent wind" that "fills the entire house" where we dwell in expectation (see Acts 2:2).

So why deny ourselves any opportunity to come aside awhile and rest on holy ground? Why not withdraw from the daily web that keeps us muddled and wound? Wordsworth's complaint is ours as well: "The world is too much with us." There is no flu shot to protect us from infection by the skepticism of the media, the greed of commerce, the alienating influence of technology. We need retreats as the deer needs the running stream.

An Invitation

This book and its companions in the *A Retreat With...* series from St. Anthony Messenger Press are designed to meet that need. They are an invitation to choose as director some of the most powerful, appealing and wise mentors our faith tradition has to offer.

Our directors come from many countries, historical

eras and schools of spirituality. At times they are teamed to sing in close harmony (for example, Francis de Sales, Jane de Chantal and Aelred of Rievaulx on spiritual friendship). Others are paired to kindle an illuminating fire from the friction of their differing views (such as Augustine of Hippo and Mary Magdalene on human sexuality). All have been chosen because, in their humanness and their holiness, they can help us grow in self-knowledge, discernment of God's will and maturity in the Spirit.

Inviting us into relationship with these saints and holy ones are inspired authors from today's world, women and men whose creative gifts open our windows to the Spirit's flow. As a motto for the authors of our series, we have borrowed the advice of Dom Frederick Dunne to the young Thomas Merton. Upon joining the Trappist monks, Merton wanted to sacrifice his writing activities lest they interfere with his contemplative vocation. Dom Frederick wisely advised, "Keep on writing books that make people love the spiritual life."

That is our motto. Our purpose is to foster (or strengthen) friendships between readers and retreat directors—friendships that feed the soul with wisdom, past and present. Like the scribe "trained for the kingdom of heaven," each author brings forth from his or her storeroom "what is new and what is old" (Matthew 13:52).

The Format

The pattern for each A Retreat With... remains the same; readers of one will be in familiar territory when they move on to the next. Each book is organized as a seven-session retreat that readers may adapt to their own schedules or to the needs of a group.

Day One begins with an anecdotal introduction called "Getting to Know Our Directors." Readers are given a telling glimpse of the guides with whom they will be sharing the retreat experience. A second section, "Placing Our Directors in Context," will enable retreatants to see the guides in their own historical, geographical, cultural and spiritual settings.

Having made the human link between seeker and guide, the authors go on to "Introducing Our Retreat Theme." This section clarifies how the guide(s) are especially suited to explore the theme and how the retreatant's spirituality can be nourished by it.

After an original "Opening Prayer" to breathe life into the day's reflection, the author, speaking with and through the mentor(s), will begin to spin out the theme. While focusing on the guide(s)' own words and experience, the author may also draw on Scripture, tradition, literature, art, music, psychology or contemporary events to illuminate the path.

Each day's session is followed by reflection questions designed to challenge, affirm and guide the reader in integrating the theme into daily life. A "Closing Prayer" brings the session full circle and provides a spark of inspiration for the reader to harbor until the next session.

Days Two through Six begin with "Coming Together in the Spirit" and follow a format similar to Day One. Day Seven weaves the entire retreat together, encourages a continuation of the mentoring relationship and concludes with "Deepening Your Acquaintance," an envoi to live the theme by God's grace, the director(s)' guidance and the retreatant's discernment. A closing section of Resources serves as a larder from which readers may draw enriching books, videos, cassettes and films.

We hope readers will experience at least one of those memorable "No wonder God loves me!" moments. And we hope that they will have "talked back" to the mentors, as good friends are wont to do.

A case in point: There was once a famous preacher who always drew a capacity crowd to the cathedral. Whenever he spoke, an eccentric old woman sat in the front pew directly beneath the pulpit. She took every opportunity to mumble complaints and contradictions—just loud enough for the preacher to catch the drift that he was not as wonderful as he was reputed to be. Others seated down front glowered at the woman and tried to shush her. But she went right on needling the preacher to her heart's content.

When the old woman died, the congregation was astounded at the depth and sincerity of the preacher's grief. Asked why he was so bereft, he responded, "Now who will help me to grow?"

All of our mentors in *A Retreat With...* are worthy guides. Yet none would seek retreatants who simply said, "Where you lead, I will follow. You're the expert." In truth, our directors provide only half the retreat's content. Readers themselves will generate the other half.

As general editor for the retreat series, I pray that readers will, by their questions, comments, doubts and decision-making, fertilize the seeds our mentors have planted.

And may the Spirit of God rush in to give the growth.

Gloria Hutchinson
Series Editor
Conversion of Saint Paul, 1995

Getting to Know Our Director

Introducing Mark

Mark begins:

My name is Mark. I am sure we have met before. I wrote the Gospel. Why they named it after me is beyond me. It is not about me at all. It is about Jesus. I am not the Good News; Jesus is. It is his Gospel. As a matter of fact, he *is* the Gospel.

Perhaps my name was attached to it because I did the actual writing. But I did not compose it, much less create it. Every jot and tittle of it came from the Church. I am not so much an author as a gatherer. I gathered the things that Jesus had said and done that I heard from the community.

If the Gospel bears my name, it is only because you will come to Jesus through my faith. I wrote this Gospel for you. Through me, I want you to touch him, to hold him, to hug him, to hear him and to become one with him. Notice that I didn't say "to know him."

As much as I like the song "Getting to Know You," I am reluctant to use "know him." That is because you Westerners have such a strange idea of knowledge. You think that when you have all the facts you know a person. That's a shame. When you have that kind of knowledge, you can respond by saying, "How interesting!" When we Jews speak of knowledge, it demands a response of yes or no. The Gospel I wrote is neither a catechism nor a biography but an invitation with an R.S.V.P. attached. That is why my friend Paul, even twenty years after his conversion, could still say, "All I want is to know Christ Jesus." He wasn't talking about the need for a sabbatical program to imbibe the Christology of twentieth-century theologian Karl Rahner. He was talking about the lifelong work and goal of a disciple: to become one with Jesus.

But you still want to know about me. Fair enough, as long as you don't think that you are becoming *my* disciple. I suppose no publisher, much less a reader, is really willing to accept writing from an author about whom they know nothing. Still, it's a strange experience. I don't recall ever having had to put together a curriculum vitae before.

Nor did I ever think that anyone would spend their lives studying what I wrote, much less who I was. But, C.E.B. Cranfield, who wrote the "Gospel According to St. Mark" in the *Cambridge Greek Testament Commentary* says: "We may take it as virtually certain that the Mark who is the associate of Peter, and the author of the Gospel and the Mark of Acts and the Pauline epistles are one and the same person."[1] Was I glad to hear that. I don't need an identity crisis.

Just a word of caution. In the early Church, I was known as the "interpreter" of Peter.[2] In going through my Gospel, you will not always be able to tell where Peter leaves off and my interpretation starts.

With this book, the same process continues. Stephen Doyle, O.F.M., is my interpreter. As in the Gospel, you may find anachronisms, inconsistencies or irregularities. Chalk it up to literary license. I just hope that he does better in English than I did in Greek.

No doubt you have read my Gospel and are wondering if the picture of the young man who lost his clothes in the garden of Gethsemane is autobiographical.[3] Keep wondering.

I lived in Jerusalem, before the Roman occupiers leveled it just as Jesus foretold.[4] My mother, Mary, was a woman of great faith, and many of the Christians used to gather at our house for prayer. It was a rather large house since we were well off. It was there, in my own home, that I met Peter, listened to him tell of his life with Jesus and answered his invitation to follow Jesus.[5] That was the first time that I had even heard that there was a gospel. Then I came to new life in Baptism, dying and rising with Jesus. Now that is the gospel at work.

I was so excited about what the Lord had done for us and that God had loved us so much that he sent his only Son, that I was caught up in the enthusiasm of Paul who had recently converted from a religion that he thought was all rules and regulations to Jesus who is the "way and the truth and the life."[6] (I was a convert, too, but Paul had much more of a flair for the dramatic.)

With a little push from my cousin Barnabas, I joined him and Paul in preaching the gospel in Cyprus and on the Greek mainland. But after a few months of intensive travel and taxing ministry, I was on the edge of burnout and decided to go home.[7] Paul was deeply disappointed that I could not keep up with him, and he let me know it. Months later when he returned to Jerusalem, he had not yet gotten it out of his system. It is not easy to live with saints.

Barnabas wanted me to go with them on the next preaching trip, but Paul was adamant that he was not going to have a namby-pamby backslider like me. He could really be tough. He just couldn't comprehend that his drive was a rare gift, and everyone did not have it.

We all agreed that feelings were running high and that our temperamental division was on the verge of becoming a countersign to the gospel. We did agree that it was better that we go our separate ways than have the gospel frustrated. When Christians are divided and at odds, it is not good news.

Barnabas and I went back to his native Cyprus, and Paul took Silas to visit the churches in Syria. This whole unpleasant affair was an eye-opener for my spiritual growth. I found out that disciples can legitimately disagree on a lot of things and still be loyal, faithful members of the community. It also helped me realize that the cross that Jesus said we would have to bear won't necessarily come from enemies. Anyhow, Paul finally got his temper under control, so I later rejoined him, and he even wrote Timothy that he now wanted me with him, since I was a help in the ministry. That may have been an attempt at an apology, but I am afraid that he was of the opinion that being an apostle means "never having to say you're sorry."

We were no sooner back together than Paul's wings were clipped. He had gotten into trouble with the Jewish authorities in Jerusalem and impetuously appealed to Caesar during his trial in Caesarea. His request was granted and off to Rome he went.[8]

Never before or since did a Christian have the golden opportunity that was now open to me. Paul was under house arrest, and by this time, Peter had also arrived in Rome. I listened to their preaching of the gospel over and over again. (This may also have been the first time in the history of the Church that the preacher was captive—and not the audience!)

However, that was not to last. When both my guides to Jesus, Peter and Paul, affirmed his Lordship with their lives, the Christian community in Rome was thrown into a disarray that resulted in a spiritual crisis. The Emperor Nero was a maniac, and his attacks on the followers of the "Way" were intensified. The mindless suffering and bloody persecution were unbelievable. Those who had come to Jesus to find hope, fulfillment, consolation and a light in the darkness were now enmeshed in fear, desperation and suffering.

Many began wondering if they should abandon the sinking ship. Where was Jesus in all of this? Following him had become unbearable. With Nero on a destructive rampage, did it make any sense at all to say, "Jesus is Lord"? Who really was in charge? Peter and Paul and I had preached that there was Good News, but that was being smothered and engulfed by the bad news. The Christians were looking to me for an answer. I gave it to them. It is called the Gospel According to Mark.

Placing Our Director in Context

The greatest graces and blessings of my life are that I came to Jesus through Peter and did my apprenticeship in evangelization with Paul. I was in Rome when the Emperor Nero left me and the Church there in chaos and confusion by martyring them both. Many began to regret their own conversions as an overly enthusiastic exercise in futility or, worse, deception. To judge from appearances, there was no doubt who was in charge, who was lord. Nero won, hands down. I quickly decided that there was no sense in everyone losing their heads, so I went on retreat. My faith assured me that Jesus was Lord, but it surely did not look like it.

Underground with other followers of Jesus, I ransacked my memory and theirs. I prayed and begged the Holy Spirit to enlighten me. Each time I secretly joined the other Christians in the "breaking of the bread" I heard the wonderful story of the death and resurrection of the Lord. I went back over my old homilies, and then I began to write. I was in a hurry since some believers were giving up, feeling that they had better abandon a sinking ship. For them Jesus was not the solution. As a matter of fact, faith in him was the problem.

The result was the first written Gospel. But it was not the last.

Matthew and Luke plagiarized me. They reworked and added to my material. No problem. They had to make it personal to their own churches, fully adapted to the situation and needs of their own communities. I don't mind their not giving me credit, but Luke could have skipped that crack about writing in "a more orderly way." So what if he did have to correct my grammar and use a more sophisticated vocabulary. The times were critical, and I was more interested in the saving power of Jesus than in literary correctness.

After all of these years, I have nothing more to say. I have a one-track mind, and Jesus is the One. He is the last word. I am still as enthusiastic and excited about him as when I first heard Peter tell about him when I was a young man in Jerusalem. That is the Gospel that I am handing on to you. As I came to know and love him through the faith of Peter and Paul, I pray that you will come to know and love him better through my faith. I wrote this Gospel with you in mind.

Notes

[1] Cranfield, C.E.B., "The Gospel According to St. Mark," *The Cambridge Greek Testament Commentary*, ed. C.F.D. Moule (New York: Cambridge University Press, 1966), p. 6.

[2] Papias (A.D. 140) quoted by Eusebius, cf. Cranfield, p. 3.

[3] Mark 14:51-52.

[4] Mark 13:2.

[5] Acts 12:12.

[6] John 14:6.

[7] Acts 12:13.

[8] Acts 26:32.

DAY ONE
Jesus: The Gospel

Introducing Our Retreat Theme

Mark continues:

I am not a politician, but I want to make one thing perfectly clear: I did not write a biography or a history book. Until my time, the gospel was a living invitation. It started with "Come, follow me." It was continued and extended in the preaching of the apostles and was written down only when they went to join Jesus in the heavenly Jerusalem.

I hope that several times while we are listening to the call of Jesus together, you will read through my Gospel in different versions. Read it as it was first preached: aloud. Would you believe that after all the work I put into it, you can still sit down and read the whole thing in less than an hour. Proclaim it. Interpret it. Go for an Academy Award. When I first heard Peter tell those stories, he was overpowered with emotion. They were remembered as much for how he said it, as what he said. Record yourself proclaiming it. Play it back. Use several versions: NAB, NRSV, NIV, NEB, NJB, or the GNB.[1] They are all good.

I was not so sure what was guiding me when I wrote my Gospel.

Now I know. The Holy Spirit was at work in the community and in me. My word is also the word of God.

It is a word of power, grace and creation. Always read the gospel with prayer, and I promise you that the same Spirit that was at work in me will be at work in you. May this retreat lead you ever closer to Jesus, for that is the only reason that there exists the Holy Gospel of Jesus Christ According to Saint Mark.

Opening Prayer

May the Lord be in my heart and on my lips, that with power and grace I may live the holy gospel, in the name of the Father and of the Son and of the Holy Spirit. Amen.

RETREAT SESSION ONE

The moment I put quill to parchment (Oh, for a word processor!) and wrote the first line, I perceived that I was on dangerous ground. The document I was writing would inevitably resemble the collections of the teachings of other great people. Documents were circulating that contained the words and deeds of Aristotle and Plato and even of Jesus' predecessors, Moses and Elijah. That similarity could be very misleading. People could mistakenly think that Jesus was just a great teacher like the rest. I tried to make clear that that was not the case.

I wrote very directly that this document was unlike any piece of literature ever written before. I cannot imagine how I could have said it more openly: The gospel *is* Jesus. Most translators miss the point entirely. They say it is the gospel *of* Jesus, which immediately leads to misunderstanding. Some will easily draw the conclusion that the teachings of Jesus are the gospel and therefore, the source of grace and life for us. They are not. Jesus is the source of grace and life. His words are an invitation to salvation, not a means to it.

To think that words can save us is to fall into the trap of those Pharisees who thought that the Law could save them. That is exactly what my friend Paul was converted from. Previously, he had thought that the Law was the source of salvation. He did not convert from "salvation by means of the Law" to "salvation by means of the teachings of Jesus." He converted to Jesus. In his own words:

> Everything I used to consider an asset has been moved over to the debit column. There is nothing, absolutely nothing, that can come close to the incredible advantage of knowing Jesus, my messiah and Lord. God's graceful love has brought me to life, not because I obeyed the commandments, but because I have been embraced by his Son, and entered into the power of his risen life.[2]

I don't mean to beat this into the ground, but the point is critical. None of the teachings of Jesus are unique to him. Even his most memorable line, that love is the most important law, is not original. He quotes it from his favorite book, Deuteronomy. One of the early Church Fathers was fond of saying that there is only one line in the entire New Testament that is totally unique: "And the Word became flesh and made his dwelling among us."[3]

My Christian community was being decimated as I wrote the Gospel. They went willingly to martyrdom, bearing witness to Jesus. They would give up everything for him who gave himself for them. But they would not have faced death just for his teachings. That's exactly what he was talking about when I quote him later on in the text[4] (8:35; 10:29; 13:10). They knew that when the Lord said, "Whoever loses his life for my sake and that of the gospel will save it," he meant that the gospel is himself and he is the gospel.

The next time I used the word, I did so twice in verses fourteen and fifteen of Chapter One: "...Jesus came to Galilee, proclaiming the gospel of God. He wants to lord it over you now. 'The time is ripe, do an about face, and sink your roots in the gospel.'"[5] (The more familiar, perhaps too familiar, translation is "Jesus came to Galilee proclaiming the gospel of God: 'This is the time of fulfillment. The kingdom of God is at hand. Repent, and believe in the gospel.'")

From what I have said, it should be no surprise to you that the words *gospel* and *Jesus* are synonyms (so with Kingdom of God, but more about that later). Therefore, when Jesus calls for faith in the gospel, he is calling for faith in himself.

I hope you know what he means by faith, but I wonder. I am a Jew like Jesus even though I wrote my Gospel and preached in the West. I know how people raised in the Greco-Roman or Western mentality love to define, conceptualize and intellectualize so that orthodoxy will be triumphant and faith will be identified with a catechism or a creed. When Jesus and I thought of faith it was not in terms of intellectual affirmation. It comes from the Hebrew word *amunah*, which is also the source of the word *amen*. It means to be firmly established, well-grounded, rooted. Faith asks the questions: Where is your center of gravity? What makes you tick?

So when Jesus says that you must believe in the gospel, he is not saying that you must assent intellectually to all the truths found in the book. He means that you must say yes to him, drop everything and follow him as the Twelve did.

Paul, with his way with words, puts it as a wonderful challenge: "Since you have accepted Jesus as your Messiah and Lord, live at one with him. Sink your roots deep in him and let faith be your solid foundation."[6]

Lest I end the first day throwing you into total chaos and confusion, let me be clear that I am not denying that there is truth and teaching in the gospel. It contains the truth of how to live out your life, united to Jesus. The people for whom I wrote had already accepted Jesus as the gospel. Now they were learning to live out the mystery of life in him. They were beginning to grasp what it means to live a gospel life. The gospel both invited them to live their lives in Jesus, and also showed them how to live out that commitment. You can appreciate why gospels are the bane of the Library of Congress and of every catalog librarian who ever lived. A gospel is in a category all by itself and does not fit in with any other category of literature.

Early in the history of the Church, there was a man whose parents obviously did not like him, since they named him Tatian. He was easily addled, for after having read the four Gospels, he decided that the "simple laity" would be confused. (You guessed it, he was a priest!) He decided to reverse the work of the Holy Spirit by ironing out the differences in the Gospels by producing only one text.

He totally missed the point that each Gospel is Jesus. But it is Jesus through the faith of the individual evangelist and his unique community under the inspiration of the Holy Spirit. What a loss if we had ended up with only one Gospel. We need all four, if I have to say so myself. My faith and the faith of my community have been a great gift, and through our faith we want to bring you Jesus.

And then what do you do? The same as we did. I recently saw a poster that tells it like it is. On it was written: "The Only Gospel Some People May Ever Read Is the One You Write With Your Life."

For Reflection

- *Have you ever stood in amazement, staring at a newborn baby? Have you been awestruck at the beauty of a bride? Do you remember being mesmerized at the sight of the Christmas tree? Those are experiences beyond words. So is the fact that Jesus loves us, came to us, gives himself for us and invites us to follow him. Mark's Gospel is an invitation. Write out your R.S.V.P.*

- *Get out your tape player and record yourself reading and interpreting Mark's Gospel. During the process, ask yourself: What new discoveries am I making about Jesus? About myself?*

- *Take the Gospel in your hands and ask God who brought light out of darkness to transform the words on the page to the Word in your heart. What Scripture passage(s) will you learn by heart during your retreat?*

- *Thank Mark for his Gospel and tell him to move over because now you will be composing your own. Can you imagine? You are going to be Good News! What feelings does this revelation arouse in you?*

Closing Prayer

Christ as a light, illumine and guide me.
Christ as a shield, o'ershadow and cover me.
Christ be before me, behind me, about me.
Christ this day be within and without me.

Christ, the lowly and the meek,

Christ, the all powerful, be in the heart of each
    to whom I speak,
In the mouth of each who speaks to me,
In all who draw near me or see me or hear me.[7]

Notes

[1] *New American Bible, New Revised Standard Version, New International Version, New English Bible, New Jerusalem Bible, Good News Bible.*

[2] Philippians 3:8-10 (author's translation).

[3] John 1:14.

[4] Mark 8:35, 10:29, 13:10.

[5] Author's translation.

[6] Colossians 2:6-7 (author's translation).

[7] Poetic adaption of part of the "Lorica," which is also called "St. Patrick's Breastplate." The text is attributed to Saint Patrick.

[handwritten notes:]

If you wrote down your own Gospel what would you say?
How do you show the gospel / Jesus to others
How do other people show the Gospel / Jesus to you.
Any clues in chapter 1?

DAY TWO
Jesus: The Call to Repent

Coming Together in the Spirit

The Japanese rarely convert to Christianity. The number of Christians in the entire country is minuscule, less than one percent. However, when they do convert, it is not because they are attracted to a new way of life or something akin to a self-help program. They convert because they are utterly amazed that "God so loved the world that he sent his only begotten Son." Every indigenous religion with which they are familiar— Shintoism, Buddhism, Taoism—are religious philosophies. They can all provide a more or less satisfying Way and Truth. But only in Jesus can they find Life. For those of us who were born into Christianity, the Japanese convert is a reminder that we may be missing what Christianity is all about, because we take for granted: "The Word was made flesh."

Defining Our Thematic Context

The movement to put Christ back into Christmas is commendable. But that is one day in three hundred and sixty-five. Perhaps we need to put Christ back into Christianity. The tendency to consider ourselves Christian because we obey the rules, affirm the beliefs, or go to church is a potent cause of self-deception. In his prologue, John states that "to those who accepted him, he gave power to become children of God, to those who believe in his name...." "Accepting him," there's the problem. We easily identify with Francis Thompson in his "Hound of Heaven":

> (For though I knew His Love who followèd,
> Yet was I sore adread
> Lest having Him, I must have naught beside.)

We fear to let go. But unless we do, we will be filled not with him, but with ourselves.

Opening Prayer

God, our Father, when we became smug, comfortable and self-satisfied, you always sent your prophets to alert us to our foolishness. May Saint Mark help us to listen more closely to the words of Jesus, your Prophet and Son. May we never take his words as less than a challenge to change our lives and follow him more deeply. Amen.

RETREAT SESSION TWO

Mark continues:

Perhaps the most dramatic conversion in the Bible is that of Paul. The Church has a feast day not only to celebrate his sainthood (with that of Peter on June 29), like all the others (including your mentor; don't forget me on April 25), but also a feast day to celebrate his renowned conversion (January 25). It was so dramatic that most people have difficulty identifying with it. Luke found it so impressive that he tells the story three times in his book, the Acts of the Apostles,[1] but it is not like anything I ever experienced.

My conversion was a slow process of saying "yes" to Jesus, whose invitation is a call to repentance. That doesn't mean "doing penance." To repent is to convert. It means to do an about-face, to make a U-turn. The recognition that you are lost or going in the wrong direction is the beginning of repentance, or conversion.

When Peter stood in the atrium of my house in Jerusalem and told us about Jesus the Risen Lord, I slowly came to the realization that Jesus was everything I had yearned for. What he had to offer was everything I was looking for, but I had been looking in the wrong places. The struggle for goodness and holiness was over. I no longer had to lead a life of frustration, trying to be a goody-goody two-shoes, by obeying six hundred and thirteen rules and regulations. All I had to do was say "yes" to Jesus and let him direct my life.

That was my conversion, or more properly, that is my conversion, for it is still going on. That is why, even though I was impressed with Paul's conversion, I was encouraged to hear him say twenty years later: "It is not that I have arrived yet, but I keep going on, trying to get my arms around him who already has his arms around me."[2]

Conversion is not the only synonym for repentance. Another is evangelization. I wrote the Gospel as a call to conversion, as a challenge to repentance. To paraphrase Jesus' words, "Repent and be evangelized."

If you read my Gospel carefully, you will find out that it is not only Jesus' invitation to conversion, but the story of those to whom he issued it. A few did the U-turn and became disciples; more preferred going in the wrong direction. I have put them in my Gospel as a challenge to you. You have to empty yourself in repentance to be filled by Jesus. You have to convert from going in the wrong direction so that you can run toward Jesus. I did.

Look at it another way. Jesus was not happy with the titles that others wanted to impose upon him, especially that of messiah. But one that he accepted as a good self-description was prophet. "Jesus said to them, 'A prophet is not without honor except in his native place and among his own kin and in his own house.'"[3]

It has been said that a prophet is one who comforts the afflicted and afflicts the comfortable. That sounds just like Jesus' job description. (As a matter of fact, if I had thought of that, I would have included it in my Gospel.)

The comfortable, of course, are those who don't think they need conversion. Self-doubt is a stranger to them, and any change is unthinkable, especially if it involves repentance. The prophets of old would zero right in on them and name them for what they were: idol worshipers. They were not so naive as to fall on their knees before brass, wood or stone. Their idols were more sophisticated. Instead of Baal, Astarte or Marduk they had names like Ego, Smugness, Arrogance, Consumerism, Snobbery, Addiction, Self-righteousness, Self-made, Self-help, Self-pity, Self-satisfied and the one with the longest name: "Weneverdiditthatwaybefore."

It has always been amazing to me that the persons who need conversion the most are the ones who think they need it least. Among them I include myself. When Peter came into our home in Jerusalem and started talking about Jesus, the last thing on my mind was repentance or conversion. I knew what sinners were and I steered clear of them. I was not about to get involved with those people who did not take religion seriously, violating the Sabbath, eating nonkosher food and other such things that I used to think God really got angry about.

Then, when I started getting involved in the literary world, I came to realize that both the Hebrew and the Greek words for sin don't refer to breaking the laws, rules and regulations. To sin is to miss the goal, to miss the mark, to go off on a tangent. That was a shocker.

I was acquainted with quite a few people who scrupulously observed all the religious precepts and rituals and were still missing the goal. God, made manifest in his Son, Jesus, is the goal of our life. Yet how many people did I meet who were so busy with religion, that they had no time for God, much less his Son. Talk about missing the point!

Please remember that when you are reading my Gospel and I tell the stories of those who criticized or tried to marginalize Jesus, it is not so that you can sit back and say: "It figures! What did you expect?" No, read the story and find out if it's autobiographical. Like David, when he heard Nathan's parable, the proper response may very well be to jump up and say: "That's me!" Then you are ready for Jesus' message: "Repent and believe in the gospel."

Just take a look at what happens. Jesus no sooner proclaims the need for repentance in Chapter One, than I had to draw up a rogues' gallery of prime candidates for repentance in Chapter Two. (Please read Chapter Two.)

I ended Chapter One with the common people caught up in enthusiasm about him. Enter the scribes. They were either lay (Pharisees) or clerical (Sadducces), but in either case they were close to the top rung on the ladder of professional religious. Intimately acquainted with the sacred writings, some of them prided themselves on knowing God's plans and *modus agendi*. They considered themselves so privy to the workings of the Divine, that they immediately recognized a fraud when they saw one.

Technically, they were correct. Only God can forgive sins. Obviously one who claims to forgive sins can be only one of two things, either God or a fraud. Since, in their experience, God did not act this way, Jesus must be a fraud. Having decided how God should act, they concluded that they had a charlatan in their midst. Their theology left no room for the God of surprises. They had their system, and God had to act according to the rules. Their system became their idol. Their preconceived notions and closed minds prevented these professional religious from being embraced by their God. The gospel was closed to them because they were too set in their ways, and their minds were locked shut.

The same group became livid when Jesus began associating with people whom God would have enough sense to shun as hopeless. Tax collectors and sinners were a whole category of pariahs who never had to be told to go to hell. The scribes had infallibly decided that the tax collectors and other sinners were well on their way. They were outside God's love. (Wasn't it convenient that his good taste coincided with their own?) Can't you just hear them boasting that they did not suffer fools gladly? They would find out who the fools were if they would only repent and believe in their way of being religious.

Jesus' next encounter was with some people who would identify well with the description of the Pilgrims made by an American historian: "They had that haunting fear that somewhere, somehow, someone would be happy." (I know that is an anachronism coming from me, but bear with me, I'm just trying to be relevant.) "Why did not Jesus and his disciples fast?" they whined. They took all the joy out of the source of all joy: life with Jesus. They were not ready for good news.

Should it be any wonder that I felt compelled to finish

the chapter with Jesus' teaching about new wine and old wineskins? Those old wineskins in his audience just would not hold his new wine. They were set in their ways, closed in their minds and narrow in their vision (and perhaps not a little nervous about losing their jobs as professional religious). Who knows what would happen if God were allowed to take over religion? We might have to repent and believe in the good news.

For Reflection

In this age of evangelization, the most insightful guide is Pope Paul VI's 1975 apostolic exhortation *Evangelii nuntiandi (Evangelization in the Modern World)*. His paragraph on the Church's need for conversion is a soul-searching challenge to each of us.

> The Church is an evangelizer, but she begins by being evangelized herself. She is the community of believers, the community of hope, lived and communicated, the community of mutual love; and she needs to listen unceasingly to what she must believe, to her reasons for hoping, to the new commandment of love. She is the people of God immersed in the world, and often tempted by idols, and she always needs to hear the proclamation of the "mighty works of God" which converted her to the Lord. She always needs to be called together afresh by him and reunited. In brief, this means that she has a constant need of being evangelized, if she wishes to retain freshness, vigor and strength to proclaim the Gospel. The Second Vatican Council recalled and the 1974 Synod vigorously took up again this theme of the Church which is evangelized by constant conversion and renewal in order to evangelize the world with credibility.[4]

- *How would you most like to see the Church evangelized today? How can you help make that evangelization a reality?*

- *In reading the Gospel of Mark, examine each of the figures whom Jesus encounters. Why did they or did they not "Repent and believe in the Gospel"? If they did not, name the idol that they could not let go of. Has it taken on another, perhaps more subtle form in your life? Explain.*

- *You are an evangelizer, but you begin by being evangelized. You are the Church immersed in the world and always tempted by idols. Locate these idols and ask God to remove you from their bondage.*

- *In 1 Corinthians 12:3 to a Church emerging from idol worship, Paul proclaims: "No one can say, 'Jesus is Lord,' except by the Holy Spirit." Who or what is the Lord of your life? Prove that the Holy Spirit is with you by praying.*

Closing Prayer

Jesus is Lord.
Jesus is Lord.
Jesus is Lord.

Notes

[1] Acts 9, 22, 26.

[2] Philippians 3:12 (author's translation).

[3] Mark 6:4.

[4] *Evangelii nuntiandi (Evangelization in the Modern World)* (Jamaica Plains, N.Y.: Daughters of St. Paul, 1976), cf. p. 58, n. 20 (19) of this book.

DAY THREE
Jesus: The Messiah

Coming Together in the Spirit

There is a splendid seminary named after John XXIII in Weston, Massachusetts, that specializes in preparing older men for the priesthood. They have been called "delayed vocations," "second-career vocations," "retreads," or "those who gave their youth to the world and their bones to the Church." During the seventeen happy years that I was on the faculty, I never ceased to be amazed at the life stories of the seminarians. Part of the admissions process was writing an autobiography. As one born and baptized into a Catholic family, who entered the seminary at age fifteen, I found their conversion stories to be eye-openers and challenges to me.

Forty years after my Baptism, they helped me to find out what it means to be a Christian. I was beginning to find out that conversion is not a once-in-a-lifetime, dramatic event, but a daily process of turning toward Jesus.

Defining Our Thematic Context

When God made us in his own image and likeness, did he realize what a precedent he was setting? Ever since

29

that moment, we have been making God into our own images and likenesses. We are tempted to think that religion is defining him in terms of our needs, and theology is describing him in terms of our expectations. If there is a tragic side to Mark's Gospel, it is not found in the life and death of Jesus. It is found in the false expectations of those who turned away when their hopes were disappointed and he did not fit into their mold.

Opening Prayer

"Master, to whom shall we go? You have the words of eternal life."[1]

RETREAT SESSION THREE

Mark continues:

When I sat down to write, the first words that came out were: "The Gospel of Jesus Christ." In our preaching, Jesus became so identified with his role of being the Christ that by the year 65, his job became part of his name. If he had been a teacher, we would have said Jesus the Teacher, not Jesus Teacher. If he had been a healer, we would have said Jesus the Healer, not Jesus Healer, as if it were his last name. But with his job of Christ (Hebrew *Messiah*), it was just so totally him and no other that it seemed natural to refer to him as Jesus Christ and not Jesus the Christ, which is more accurate.

That usage was bad and good for later generations. It was bad because later generations became woefully ignorant of Jesus' Bible, which they then proceeded to make irrelevant by calling it the "Old Testament." That Bible was a major source of Jesus' spirituality, and those who don't know it will be sadly ignorant of Jesus himself. If they don't know what are properly called the "Hebrew Scriptures," how will they know what it means to call Jesus Messiah?

Calling him Jesus Christ has its good side, though. My community used those Scriptures. They were our only Bible, and in them we searched for "he who is to come." In my day, every pious Jew was a person of hope. We were future-oriented. What God had done, he would do. His past actions were not just to be marveled at. They contained a promise. His message to Moses was that he was troubled by the suffering of his people and chose Moses to join him in bringing about their liberation.

Later on, the system of government changed from the autocratic rule of Moses, and the charismatic but chaotic rule of the judges to the monarchy of David and the anointed kings (messiahs) descended from him. The establishment of messiahship was not the result of a profound revelation of the divine plan. It sprang from a political pragmatism vividly portrayed at the end of the Book of Judges and the beginning of the First Book of Samuel. Some changes in the leadership structure had to occur if the community was to survive and not pass into oblivion. Idolatry, rape, genocide and selfishness were tearing the community apart. If it was to survive as God's people, the community needed a messiah to keep it from disintegrating.

The role of the messiah was to identify, confront and deal with those problems that threatened the health or the very survival of the community. Thus was born the concept of messianic hope or promise. But the perception of the nature of the problem colored that hope. The job description of each hoped-for messiah was written by the troubled community. If they decided, as they did in the time of Jesus, that the occupation of their nation by the Roman army was the chief obstacle to their living as God's people, then they prayed for a messiah to lead a military insurrection. If a messiah came along who refused to accept their job description, he was unacceptable and considered an impostor.

Jesus was the Messiah, but he wasn't their kind of messiah. That was the biggest problem he faced. They had false hopes because they had not put their finger on their real problem. And once they had missed the point as to the nature of their problem, the next step was to search the Scriptures for texts that would support their misplaced expectations. Anything about David, the warrior, victor or conqueror, would do. Psalm 2 was their rallying cry:

> I myself have set up my king
> on Zion, my holy mountain....
> Ask of me and I will give you
> the nations for an inheritance
> and the ends of the earth for your possession.
> You shall rule them with an iron rod;
> you shall shatter them like an earthen dish.[2]

Once blinded by their own hopes and expectations, they had nothing but contempt for anyone who was thought to be a messiah and fell short of those hopes and expectations. Of course, for Jesus, it was a ready-made trap. He was the Messiah, but not according to their standards. He tried to avoid the trap as much as he could by demanding silence and secrecy of those whom he healed, or of those to whom he manifested the power that God was expected to work through his Messiah. He did manifest that power time and time again, but he had to avoid giving to his contemporaries the impression that it was a foretaste of the military power that they yearned for.

He would be a messiah, but on his terms, not theirs.

I hope you don't feel that I have been belaboring this point. It was critical in the life of Jesus and in my generation following his. It is pivotal for you as well. To be his disciple is to follow him as he is, not as you want him to be. That is the very reason for writing my Gospel. My community in Rome, like his own generation in Judea, wanted a messiah, but without the cross. Don't we all? We would all prefer a Mr. Fixit who would provide the solution to every problem that we present to him.

Notice how I tried to emphasize the point in my Gospel. "The Pharisees came forward and began to argue with him, seeking from him a sign from heaven to test him. He sighed from the depth of his spirit and said, 'Why does this generation seek a sign? Amen, I say to you, no sign will be given to this generation.'"[3]

The Pharisees wanted proof that Jesus had been sent by God as an answer to their prayers. Since their prayers were for the wrong kind of messiah, no sign would have convinced them. That becomes more evident when we realize that Jesus had just multiplied the loaves, a messianic sign from the time of Moses who gave the people bread (manna) in the desert.[4] If they could not recognize a sign from God, how would they expect to recognize the Messiah from God? "No sign will be given to this generation."

At least Jesus could count on his intimate friends, couldn't he? "Along the way he asked his disciples, 'Who do people say that I am?' They said in reply, 'John the Baptist, others Elijah, still others one of the prophets.' And he asked them, 'But who do you say that I am?' Peter said to him in reply, 'You are the Messiah.' Then he warned them not to tell anyone about him."[5]

He not only pledged them to secrecy, but decided to let them in on the secret of his real job description as messiah. "...[T]he Son of Man must suffer greatly and be rejected by the elders, the chief priests, and the scribes, and be killed, and rise after three days."[6]

Being a product of his generation and sharing his generation's hopes, Peter has a better idea. He and the gang can save Jesus from such a fate. Jesus is far from pleased. Even his intimate friends won't let him be what he has to be and do what he has to do. Even by violence, they would force him into the mold of their own expectations and desires. "Get behind me, Satan. You are thinking not as God does, but as human beings do."[7] Strong language to the first pope from the Messiah!

And to make sure that they did not misunderstand his role as messiah, Jesus immediately let them know that the same fate was in store for them. They had the same job description. "Whoever wishes to follow me must deny himself, take up his cross and follow me."[8]

When the stories about Jesus came down to me, they came without calendar or map. Very often I did not know when or where they occurred, and, by the time I began writing, Peter had been martyred. I was free to arrange the sayings and deeds of Jesus as I thought best. I decided that this would be a perfect place, after Peter's confession and Jesus' job description of himself and his followers, to put the story of the Transfiguration. I'll tell you why.

Look back at the events leading up to this point in the life of the Messiah. In Chapter Six, the Baptist is beheaded and Herod thinks he has come back to life as Jesus. At Nazareth, both family and neighbors dismiss Jesus as a fraud. After all, they knew him when!

When Jesus raises Jairus' daughter, he is ridiculed. When he manifests the breaking in of the Kingdom of God by casting out Satan, the elite theologians from Jerusalem accuse him of promoting the kingdom of Satan. His family comes to protect him from himself because they think he is mad. He cures people and is charged with being an irreligious Sabbath-breaker. He eats with tax collectors and sinners and is judged not to be in the proper company for a messiah. He forgives sins and is charged with blasphemy.

The voices of ridicule, suspicion, condemnation and enmity are bursting around him like the waves of the sea: "Nonobservant Jew, hick from Galilee trying to teach his betters, layman who has no respect for the religious authorities." He's a loser who doesn't even know how the Messiah is supposed to act. He doesn't have a clue about what Moses and the prophets said the Messiah would be like. If his followers had any sense, they'd abandon this cause and get on with their lives.

Jesus had not lost sight of what kind of messiah he was to be. Those around him made sure that his expectation of being a suffering messiah was met. But Peter, so recently told to go to the devil along with the other disciples, must have been thrown into doubt and indecision by the negative voices. A retreat on a high mountain away from the crowd was in order. I don't know how long they stayed, but if Tabor is the mountain, they didn't climb it just to make a holy hour.

It must have been a time of prayer and discernment as Jesus led them to see that the course he was following was in the tradition of two of the great leaders of God's people, Moses and Elijah. Peter, James and John came to realize that his was the authentic voice of messianic fulfillment and not the cacophony of voices that they had been listening to down below. Moses and Elijah put the seal of approval on him, and it was confirmed by the voice from heaven: "This is my beloved Son. Listen to him."

It was not easy for me to write about a suffering messiah. It doesn't make a lot of sense to people who are looking for a messiah who will take away suffering. It looks like consummate foolishness. Paul helped me put this in perspective: "...Jews demand signs and Greeks look for wisdom, but we proclaim Christ [the Messiah] crucified, a stumbling block to Jews and foolishness to Gentiles, but to those who are called, Jews and Greeks alike, Christ [the Messiah] the power of God and the wisdom of God. For the foolishness of God is wiser than human wisdom, and the weakness of God is stronger than human strength."[9]

For Reflection

- *Jesus' contemporaries loved Psalms 2 and 110, which are "Messianic Psalms," because a literalist interpretation of them coincided with their own ambitions and expectations. This is a good example of how a fundamentalist interpretation of the Bible can be insulting to God and misleading to us. Reflect on these psalms and ask yourself: What images of Jesus do I find in these royal coronation songs? How does he exert his princely power in my life?*

- *When I taught at Pope John XXIII Seminary for delayed vocations, the seminarians, many years away from the books, would get nervous at exam time. Thoughts of their youthful rivalry with their classmates and their competition for class standing would resurface. An astute academic dean told them: "You don't have to strive to live up to anyone's expectations except God's, and you are not competing with anyone but yourself." How might these words apply to Jesus' messianic vocation? Are there ways in which you might apply them to your own life? Explain.*

- *Contrary to all expectations and hopes, Jesus chose the way of the cross. Make it with him, and at the twelfth station, look up at him and pray: "Jesus, did you do that just for me?"*

Closing Prayer

And when I think that God his Son not sparing
Sent him to die, I scarce can take it in.
That on the cross, my burden gladly bearing,
He bled and died to take away my sin.

Then sings my soul, my Saviour God to thee,
How great thou art, how great thou art.[10] (Repeat)

Christ Jesus Lord, you rose that Easter morn,
And to your friends, you came to show the way.
Shalom my gift, again I say Shalom,
Abba's Spirit is yours this blessed day.[11]

Then sings my soul, my Saviour God to thee,
How great thou art, how great thou art. (Repeat)

Notes

[1] John 6:68b.
[2] Psalm 2:6, 8, 9.
[3] Mark 8:11-12.
[4] John 6:30-31.
[5] Mark 8:27b-30.
[6] Mark 8:31.
[7] Mark 8:33b.
[8] Mark 8:34b.
[9] 1 Corinthians 1:22-25.
[10] Words by Stuart K. Hine.
[11] Words by Stephen C. Doyle, O.F.M.

DAY FOUR

Jesus: The Son of Man

Coming Together in the Spirit

One of my professors once wrote what is probably the shortest book review ever written: "There has long been a need for a book like this. The need remains."

Just the opposite is true of Jaroslav Pelikan's *Jesus Through the Centuries: His Place in the History of Culture* (Harper and Row, New York, 1985). Whatever Pelikan writes can be counted on to be worthwhile, but this book is superb. In eighteen chapters, he looks at Jesus against the culture, philosophy, theology, politics and religion of the last twenty centuries. Truly, Jesus emerges as a man for all seasons—yesterday, today and forever.

However, none of those images of Jesus in the last twenty centuries would have been possible without the humble and lowly portrait that Mark gives us in the first century. Without Mark's faith and that of his fellow disciples who handed on the stories about Jesus, we'd probably still be prostrating ourselves before golden calves. Instead, we have good news, news of the Word who was made flesh and dwelt among us, and to as many as received him, he gave the power to become the children of God. (See Prologue of the Gospel of Saint John.)[1]

Defining Our Thematic Context

Mark begins and ends his Gospel with the affirmation that Jesus is the "Son of God" (1:1; 15:39). And every line in between is an affirmation that he is the Son of Man.

The reality of the two natures, divine and human in one person, is called the Hypostatic Union. If that is a mouthful for you, you are in good company. Mark would have had to struggle to pronounce it, let alone explain it. Yet, he started it. The early councils of the Church that wrestled with the nature and meaning of Christ would have had nothing to keep theologians and bishops busy if it had not been for the first evangelist. In the process of inviting us to discipleship, Mark tells us a great deal about the God-Man, Jesus Christ.

Opening Prayer

The angel of the Lord declared unto Mary
And she conceived by the Holy Spirit.
 Hail Mary...
"Behold the handmaid of the Lord."
"Be it done unto me according to your word."
 Hail Mary...
And the Word was made flesh
And dwelt among us.
 Hail Mary...

Pray for us, O Holy Mother of God,
That we may be made worthy of the promises of Christ.[2]

RETREAT SESSION FOUR

Mark continues:

Jesus (Hebrew *Yeshua*) means "Yahweh saves," and he certainly lived up to the promise of his name. But, as I was gathering the stories and sayings of Jesus that came down to me, and interpreting them and arranging them to form the Gospel, I was fascinated by how Jesus shied away from the title Messiah and delighted in using Son of Man. He used it to refer to himself—and did you notice?—only Jesus uses it. No one calls him "Son of Man." Even when Peter gives the litany of whom people think he might be, Son of Man is not included. Obviously, no one was looking for a Son of Man.

His contemporaries, even the sectarians at Qumran, breathlessly yearning for God's judgment, make no mention of a Son of Man. It is found in the Book of Daniel, a cry of propaganda, rallying support for the Maccabean uprising against the Syrians, about one hundred and fifty years before Jesus. Among other despicable acts, the Syrian tyrant had demanded worship of an idol of himself.

It was erected in the Holy of Holies of the Temple in Jerusalem and was referred to by the faithful as the "Abomination of the Desolation." It seemed as if the dark powers of this world had backed God into a corner. How long would the Creator tolerate this reversion of his creation to chaos? Have you ever had one of those really bad days when someone says, "Cheer up, things could be worse"; so you cheer up, and sure enough, things get worse? If so, you know how bad things were a century and a half before Jesus lived.

As a sign of hope and God's definitive intervention against the powers of darkness, Daniel saw

One like a son of man coming,
  on the clouds of heaven;
When he reached the Ancient One
  and was presented before him,
He received dominion, glory, and kingship;
  nations and peoples of every language
  serve him.
His dominion is an everlasting dominion
  that shall not be taken away,
  his kingship shall not be destroyed.[3]

Jesus, who refused to see himself as smashing Israel's political enemies, did see himself as the sign of the Kingdom of God, vindicating God's justice over the powers of darkness in the end times. However, his followers will be gauged not by the amount of blood on their swords but by their fidelity to him and to his Word. "Whoever is ashamed of me and of my words in this faithless and sinful generation, the Son of Man will be ashamed of when he comes in his Father's glory with the holy angels."[4]

I noticed that in most of the stories about Jesus that were being passed on in my community that he doesn't very often use Son of Man in the triumphal sense found in the Book of Daniel. I suppose that it was as open to misunderstanding as was the title messiah. Much more often he uses "Son of Man" as found in the Book of Ezekiel to refer to himself as one of us. When God calls Ezekiel "Son of Man," God wants him to be aware that he is a member of a lowly, wounded, helpless community, the same community of which you and I are members.

The contemporaries of Jesus did not like that. They did not want a messiah so much like themselves. They wanted a triumphant victor, and Jesus presented himself as a wounded healer. He did promise that victory would come: "And then they will see 'the Son of Man coming in the clouds' with great power and glory, and then he will send out the angels and gather [his] elect from the four winds, from the end of the earth to the end of the sky."[5] But between now and then, the already and the not-yet, there is the struggle of his followers to be faithful and holy in the midst of a faithless and sinful generation.

In none of the stories that I wove into my written Gospel, does Jesus even hint that to be his follower means to escape from this world or flee from this generation. Much less does it mean to slough off the weakness and vulnerability of being human. Two affirmations of my Gospel are that Jesus is "Son of God" and "Son of Man."

How can that be? I leave to those with higher IQ's than my own to figure that out. But I believe that Jesus is Son of God and Son of Man because I heard it from Peter and Paul and others in the community. My faith is built on theirs. And from what they told me, never once did he use his being Son of God as an escape valve to avoid the pressures of being Son of Man. Never once did I hear a story of him working a miracle for himself. Right to his final moment on the cross he firmly resisted that temptation: "'Aha! You who would destroy the temple and rebuild it in three days, save yourself by coming down from the cross.'...'Let the Messiah, the King of Israel, come down now from the cross that we may see and believe.'"[6]

Read my Gospel and look for the signs of how fully and unreservedly, he, the Son of God embraced becoming Son of Man. If you recognize his weakness, struggles, frustrations and disappointments as your own, then you will recognize how much like yourself he was (and is!). When Jesus came down the mountain from the Transfiguration, he quickly brought his disciples down to earth about his role: "...how is it written regarding the Son of Man that he must suffer greatly and be treated with contempt?"[7] If this is a prediction, it is a prediction based on experience. The Son of Man has already been condemned for his table fellowship,[8] gotten angry at his critics' hardness of heart,[9] and been accused of insanity by his relatives[10] and of being in league with Satan by the religious "experts."[11] And that is only a smattering from two chapters!

Is it any wonder that every once in a while he used the only escape hatch available to him to get away from the crowds, both friendly and hostile? "He told the disciples to have a boat ready for him because of the crowd, so they would not crush him."[12] "A very large crowd gathered around him so that he got into a boat on the sea and sat down."[13] What I am saying is that, every once in a while, Jesus was so like you that he, too, felt the need for a retreat. He knows where you are and what you are going through. He is no stranger to your needs. After all, he is the Son of Man.

For Reflection

- *What Jesus affirms by taking the title Son of Man and what Mark spells out in the details of his life among us, the author of Hebrews affirms unequivocally: "...[H]e had to become like his brothers in every way, that he might be a merciful and faithful high priest before God to expiate the sins of the people"[14] and "For we do not have a high priest who is unable to sympathize with our weaknesses, but one who has similarly been tested in every way, yet without sin."[15] No Gospel gives us details of Jesus' appearance. But these texts assure us that the best way to find out what he was like is to look in the mirror. Name some of the resemblances to Jesus that you see in yourself.*

44

- *A cartoon showed a blond-haired, pink-cheeked lad wearing a crown, a satin dress and a velvet cape with a lace ruffle about his neck. The Blessed Mother leans over and says to him: "I don't care who you are, you are not going out to play dressed like that." How do you think religious art has colored, if not warped, our image of Jesus so that he becomes someone we cannot identify with? Seek a contemporary depiction of Jesus that helps you relate to him as Son of Man.*

- *An unrealistic spirituality has often affirmed that Jesus is perfect man. Wrong, if that means there is any part of our humanity except sin that he did not assume. Better to say he is perfectly and completely human. He did not take upon himself some ideal human nature that could have won a Hollywood Oscar for design. God sent "his own Son in the likeness of sinful flesh."[16]*

Closing Prayer

By the mystery of this water and wine
may we share in the divinity of Christ
who humbled himself to share in our humanity.[17]

Notes

[1] John 1:14, 12.
[2] The Angelus, a traditional Catholic prayer said at noon.
[3] Daniel 7:13-14.
[4] Mark 8:38 (Emphasis added).
[5] Mark 13:26.
[6] Mark 15:29ff.
[7] Mark 9:12.
[8] Mark 2:16.

[9] Mark 3:5.
[10] Mark 3:21.
[11] Mark 3:22.
[12] Mark 3:9.
[13] Mark 4:1b.
[14] Hebrews 2:17.
[15] Hebrews 4:15.
[16] Romans 8:3.
[17] Order of Mass (*Ordo Missae*), *The Sacramentary*, trans. International Committee on English in the Liturgy (New York: Catholic Book Publishing Co., 1985), p. 370.

DAY FIVE
Jesus: The Caller of Disciples

Coming Together in the Spirit

Menachem Schneerson, the Lubavitcher Rebbe, died recently at an advanced age in Brooklyn. Some of his more zealous disciples have taken it upon themselves to declare that he is the Messiah. In the departure lounge at the Tel Aviv airport, as well as in the Jewish Quarter of Jerusalem, portraits of him abound, with the title underneath: "Messiah King." The enthusiasm of his followers is unbridled as they await his return in triumph.

The vast majority of Israelis have other ideas. The observant disciples of other rabbis think his followers are fools. The majority of the people either pay no attention or smile at the naïveté of the religious fanatics.

As the French say: *"Plus ça change, plus c'est la meme chose."* ("The more things change, the more they remain the same.")

Defining Our Thematic Context

The story of the multiplication of the loaves and fishes[1] is amazing for many reasons: the concern of Jesus, the sheer numbers involved, the amount of food left over, etc. But it is so overwhelming that one small line that makes a major point is overlooked. When the disciples first present the problem to Jesus, his reply is: "You give them something to eat." They could not do a thing. They were obviously helpless. Their impotence in the face of his challenge must have made them feel useless.

That is exactly what Jesus intended. If they accomplished anything at all, it was not by their own ability, but by his power at work in them. Jesus did not choose the most talented, as the other rabbis did. He chose the least likely, and that is why they were successful.

Opening Prayer

Father, Mary became the first disciple of your Son when she spoke her fiat. Be it done unto me according to your word. With her you "chose us in him, before the foundation of the world." Through her prayer, may we fulfill your eternal plan as his disciples.

Pray for us, O Holy Mother of God,
That we may be made worthy of the promises of Christ.

RETREAT SESSION FIVE

Mark continues:
The titles *rabbi* and *disciple* go together. Where you find disciples, you will find a rabbi and vice versa. Even though Jesus is rarely addressed as rabbi, his followers are invariably called disciples. To my contemporaries, that title had certain definite characteristics and implications.

Everyone knew what was expected of a rabbi's disciples, how they came to be apprenticed, what their responsibilities were, what the process involved was and how long that process lasted.

I can tell you about it from experience, since I became a disciple of Jesus. And there is a world of difference between being a disciple of Jesus and being the disciple of a rabbi. I know. And you should know so that you will have no doubt about what it means to be a disciple of Jesus.

The difference starts at the very beginning. Usually, a young man would choose the most prestigious and influential rabbi to attach himself to. He did this in order to bask in the glory of his teacher.

With Jesus it is just the opposite. It is he who chooses. It is he who says, "Come, follow me." His followers did not go shopping for the rabbi most likely to succeed.

And when the rabbis accepted candidates from those who chose them, they accepted only the best and the brightest. They wanted men of promise. Their reputations depended on their disciples. They did not want to take any chances with that prized possession. Family background, status and honor were major factors in the decision.

It appears that Jesus went out of his way to ignore all such criteria. The disciples he chose would not even have merited a reply to their request for an application to rabbinical school. In your own era, their SASEs (self-addressed stamped envelopes) would have come back empty. Country-bumpkin fishermen, women and tax collectors of questionable loyalty to both religion and nation were hardly prime candidates for discipleship with a rabbi who had any self-respect.

The principal function of a rabbi's disciple was to memorize the opinion of his teacher, and then, by astute and sometimes convoluted argumentation, to prove that his mentor was the authority par excellence. Memory was of the essence. If it were not accurate down to the last detail, the rabbi could be made a fool of.

But Jesus' disciples could not even grasp the point of a simple parable. "Jesus said to them, 'Do you not understand this parable? Then how will you understand any of the parables?'"[2] "Do you still not understand?"[3] "But they did not understand the saying, and they were afraid to question him."[4] Any reputable rabbi would have flunked them. Jesus did not. And he did not simply because he had not chosen them for their dazzling IQ's or photographic memories. He chose them so that they would recognize him as the Way, the Truth and the Life.

Another major difference between the disciples of the rabbis and the disciples of Jesus is in their attitude toward the Law. The contrast could not be more vivid than in the story of the hungry disciples of Jesus munching some grain that they had just plucked from a field on a Sabbath. An observant Jew might judge the piety of other Jews by their observance of the 613 precepts of the Law. And the prime, pivotal, gauge is Sabbath observance.

Thus, the disciple of a rabbi was not only to memorize the minutiae of legal disputes, but to practice them meticulously as well. The challenge that Jesus lays down to his critics is also an instruction for his disciples: "The sabbath was made for man, not man for the sabbath."[5] His principle for them to follow was that human values take precedence over a law even as important as that of Sabbath observance.

But Jesus went further than any rabbi ever dared. A rabbi might come up with convoluted opinions that would show his disciples how to get around the law. For example, the regulation for the Sabbath was to keep it holy. This was also specified to exclude work. Then it had to be decided how far one might travel from home before it became work. Then it was decreed that home is where you eat, so that if you wanted to travel twice the permissible distance you had to carry a picnic lunch to eat halfway to your destination, thus, establishing a home. Jesus cut through it all for his disciples by the declaration: "[T]he Son of Man is lord even of the sabbath."[6] No wonder they exclaimed that he spoke as one having authority.

For the disciples of many rabbis, the Law was everything. Their enthusiasm caused them to exaggerate its importance and fail to recognize its limitations. The hyperbole of the Law's praise in the poetry of the Book of Baruch echoed their own sentiments:

> Hear, O Israel, the commandments of life:
>   listen, and know prudence!
> ...
>
> Learn where prudence is,
>   where strength, where understanding;
> That you may know also
>   where are length of days, and life,
>   where light of the eyes, and peace.[7]
> ...
>
> She is the book of the precepts of God,
>   the law that endures forever;
> All who cling to her will live,
>   but those will die who forsake her.[8]

These are words that could be applied to grace or God's love, or Jesus, but they are a misleading hyperbole when applied to the Law. Jesus knew that the Law was a gift to point the way to God. He also knew that a major limitation was that it could only affect externals and not touch the heart. It is a wonder that he ever made it to Calvary, considering how he lashed out at the Pharisees and scribes about their attitude to the Law. But, he saved his most severe critique of their practice for when he was alone with his disciples.

> When he got home away from the crowd his disciples questioned him.... He said to them, "Are even you likewise without understanding? Do you not realize that everything that goes into a person from outside cannot defile, since it enters not the heart but the stomach and passes out into the latrine?" (Thus he declared all foods clean.) "But what comes out of a person, that is what defiles. From within people, from their hearts, come evil thoughts, unchastity, theft, murder, adultery, greed, malice, deceit, licentiousness, envy, blasphemy, arrogance, folly. All these evils come from within and they defile."[9]

The disciples of the rabbis came to hear the same old traditions rehashed over and over again. Jesus thought that another prophet long ago had categorized them very well, and he was in full agreement when he quoted Isaiah against them:

> This people honors me with their lips,
>   but their hearts are far from me;
> In vain do they worship me,
>   teaching as doctrine human precepts.[10]

It was the sterile antiquarianism of the rabbis and their disciples that led him to categorize them as old wineskins that would burst with his new wine. His disciples must be open, receptive, flexible and adaptable, like new wineskins into which he could pour his new wine.

Let me give you a personal example of that flexibility and openness to adaptation that Jesus wanted us, his disciples, to have.

Remember the story about marriage and divorce when the Pharisees tried to entrap him?[11] Among the Jews, divorce was a male prerogative, and so Jesus' answer alluded only to a man divorcing his wife. But my parishioners were Romans and, according to the law of the empire, a woman could divorce her husband. I felt perfectly free to adapt the teaching of Jesus to this new situation and have Jesus say: "...and if she divorces her husband and marries another, she commits adultery."[12] A disciple of a rabbi would have been expelled and blackballed for doing what I did.

Another major difference concerns the demands that a rabbi put on his disciples. The only hardship they had to endure was burning the midnight oil while they exhausted themselves memorizing the brilliant and subtle distinctions of their mentor. The only demands placed upon them were those of academia. And that was only for a time. The stress would come to an end. They would thank their rabbi, depart, and as rabbis themselves, form groups of their own disciples, starting the cycle over.

On the contrary, the demands upon Jesus' disciples were neither partial nor temporary. His invitation was not that they pay attention to him, but that they follow him. And that following included denying themselves and taking up a cross.[13] No rabbi ever made such total demands on his disciples.

Also, no disciple of Jesus expected to or actually did graduate and begin to attract disciples of his own. My own discipleship is a prime example. I never have expected, nor do I ever expect to cease being a disciple of Jesus. If I were a disciple of a rabbi, I would not have written a Gospel but a flattering biography of my hero who set me on the path to calling my own disciples. Instead, I have written an invitation to enter into or deepen your discipleship with Jesus. You are a Christian, not a Markan.

In one way, the disciples of the rabbis and of Jesus were very similar. They both had one-track minds. But the former were preoccupied with the Law of God, while the latter were preoccupied with the Kingdom of God, for that was the burden of Jesus' own preaching. Jesus' disciples never had to wonder what they were going to preach about next Sunday. There was only one topic: the Kingdom of God.

As with all the deepest mysteries of life, words fall short when they try to express the meaning of the Kingdom of God. Mysteries, of course, cannot be defined. They can only be penetrated by story, analogy and parable. That is why Jesus never says that the Kingdom of God is..., but rather, the Kingdom of God is like.... Jesus told you what it is like in his words. As one of his disciples, let me tell you what it is like in my words. It is like finding your center of gravity. It is like receiving a corneal transplant so that now you see things through the eyes of God. It is like emerging from chaos into creation. It is like a light shining in darkness. It is like rising from death to life. It is like being embraced by the power of God. It is knowing Jesus.

You realize, of course, that Peter was a friend of mine. To him I owe my call to discipleship. I would do anything to be able to omit from the gospel of Jesus that embarrassing story of his denial.[14] But I can't, since it contains a critical lesson for the disciple. Peter was a Jew, and he was speaking Aramaic. From both points of view, the semitic mentality and language, to know does not mean being conversant with facts, details or vital statistics. "To know" another is to become one with that person. Peter is not denying that he ever met Jesus. He is not denying that he was an acquaintance of his. He is denying that Jesus had any meaningful influence on him. He is denying that their lives, goals, values and priorities ever coincided. He is denying discipleship.

As sad as that may be, my fellow disciples for whom I

was writing in Rome knew that denial was not the end of the story for Peter, just as the cross was not the end of the story for Jesus. They had heard Peter himself tell his story to let us all know that no matter how stupid, foolish or treacherous we may have been, Jesus never gives up on us. Even when we have fallen in denial, we can still hear that voice whispering in our ear: "Come, follow me!"

For Reflection

- *Mark's mentor in going forth and calling the world to discipleship was Paul. He knew the difference between a disciple of a rabbi and a disciple of Jesus. He had been both.*

Circumcised on the eighth day, of the race of Israel, of the tribe of Benjamin, a Hebrew of Hebrew parentage, in observance of the law a Pharisee, in zeal I persecuted the church, in righteousness based on the law I was blameless.

[But] whatever gains I had, these I have come to consider a loss because of Christ. More than that, I even consider everything as a loss because of the supreme good of knowing Christ Jesus my Lord. For his sake I have accepted the loss of all things and I consider them so much rubbish, that I may gain Christ and be found in him, not having any righteousness of my own based on the law but that which comes through faith in Christ, the righteousness from God, depending on faith, to know him and the power of his resurrection and [the] sharing of his sufferings by being conformed to his death. ...It is not that I have already taken hold of it or have already attained perfect maturity, but I continue my pursuit in hope that I may possess it, since I indeed have been taken possession of by Christ [Jesus].[15]

What gains and losses has any discipleship entailed? How have I allowed Jesus to take possession of me?

■ *If you are already familiar with Mark's Gospel, then you will have noticed that this treatment of discipleship has not touched on the obvious text of Mark 6:8-9. "He instructed them to take nothing for the journey but a walking stick— no food, no sack, no money in their belts. They were, however, to wear sandals but not a second tunic."*

The fact is that this is not to be taken as literal instruction on what to pack for the journey. (The parallel passages in Matthew and Luke forbid even a walking stick!) This is a visual and vivid statement of the spirit of poverty that discipleship with Jesus presupposes. It is the challenge thrown out by Jesus in the story of the rich young man.[16] "Jesus looked round and said to his disciples, 'How hard it is for those who have wealth to enter the kingdom of God.'"[17] In what ways am I already practicing the spirit of poverty Jesus requires of his disciples? How might I further simplify my material needs?

■ *The movie* Yentl *is a memorable example of a woman who wanted to be a disciple of a rabbi so that she could study Torah. Only by the ruse of disguising herself as a male was the path opened to her. Mark portrays a female disciple in the woman who anticipated the anointing of the body of Jesus for burial, of whom he said: "Amen, I say to you, wherever the gospel is proclaimed to the whole world, what she has done will be told in memory of her."[18] No less remarkable is Mark's including by name the disciples who remained faithful at the cross, all women! "Among them were Mary Magdalene, Mary the mother of the younger James and of Joses, and Salome. These women had followed him when he was in Galilee and ministered to him. There were also many other women who had come up with him to Jerusalem."[19] How does my own attitude and example help others in the Church mirror Jesus' acceptance of women as equals among his disciples?*

- *To this day, orthodox Jewry sees assimilation as the greatest danger to its own survival. Conservative and Reform Jews are castigated for their adaptations and are literally excommunicated. The Law is a wall that preserves identity and no part of it, no matter how antiquated or irrelevant, is dispensable.*

  Jesus inculcated in his disciples a sense of flexibility and a conviction that adaptation is intrinsic to the gospel. His disciples could sink their roots in any culture. That is why we have four Gospels imaging the one gospel. Peter and Paul transplanted the gospel from the Jewish to the gentile world. Mark continued to adapt it for his Roman community. That same spirit of adaptation was continued in our own lifetime by Vatican Council II.

  Pope Paul VI saw adaptation as an integral part of evangelization, with one caution:

  The question is a delicate one. Evangelization loses much of its force and effectiveness if it does not take into consideration the actual people to whom it is addressed, if it does not use their language, their signs and symbols, if it does not answer the questions they ask and if it does not have an impact on their concrete life. But on the other hand, evangelization risks losing its power and disappearing altogether if one empties or adulterates its content under the pretext of translating it.[20]

Think of how far the Church has come in the last century and how much change has taken place. Do you think the gospel has been watered down in the modern era?

Closing Prayer

At the ordination of a priest or the final profession of a religious, the candidate lies prostrate while the community of disciples surrounding them begs the prayers of the community of disciples (saints) who have gone before the candidate. Compose your own litany of saints, who are supporting you as you respond to Jesus' call to discipleship. Then kneel or lie down and pray it from your heart.

Notes

1 Mark 6:34ff.
2 Mark 4:13.
3 Mark 8:21.
4 Mark 9:32.
5 Mark 2:27b.
6 Mark 2:28.
7 Baruch 3:9ff.
8 Baruch 4:1.
9 Mark 7:17-23.
10 Mark 7:6-7.
11 Mark 10:1ff.
12 Mark 10:12.
13 Mark 8:34.
14 Mark 14:66-72.
15 Philippians 3:5-12.
16 Mark 10:17ff.
17 Mark 10:23.
18 Mark 14:9.
19 Mark 15:40b-41.
20 Pope Paul VI, *Evangelii nuntiandi* (*Evangelization in the Modern World*), #63.2

DAY SIX

Jesus: The Suffering Servant

Coming Together in the Spirit

Mark might not like being identified with "evangelists" today any more than Jesus enjoyed being identified with "messiahs" in his day. Contemporary evangelists seem very much interested in predicting the end of the world, the parousia and the rapture. They love speculating about all those things that concern the end times. They seem to be experts on reading the signs and interpreting the catastrophes of apocalyptic literature that indicate that the end is near. They seem to imply that they have an insider's knowledge of things that Jesus himself said he had no knowledge of.[1]

Evangelists of this ilk seem to justify Karl Marx's critique of religion as the opium of the people. By promising people ultimate prosperity, they distract people from the sufferings of this world and keep them drugged with the promise of pie in the sky, by and by. Their "good news" is that, for a substantial donation to their ministry, you will be rewarded by Jesus with everything from stock options to a Mercedes. Just to reinforce their point, they often drive around in one.

But when Mark recorded the promises of rewards that Jesus made to Peter, he did not leave out the last reward: persecution.[2] Somehow contemporary evangelists miss that one. Mark did not, for he knew that persecution is but a facet of the cross, and without the cross, there is no Jesus.

Defining Our Thematic Context

In Chapters 40 to 55 of the Book of Isaiah, haunting glimpses appear of the mysterious and elusive figure called the suffering servant. Among the many questions I will propose to God when I enter heaven (Is that presumption?) will be: "Who wrote these chapters?" (The poor author has been stuck with the label of Deutero-Isaiah.) And who did the author or authors have in mind as the suffering servant? He sounds like Abraham. He sounds like Moses. He sounds like David. He sounds like Jeremiah. He sounds like Israel.

But above all, the early Church recognized that suffering servant sounded like Jesus. Quotes from the suffering servant's story in the Gospels of Matthew and Luke are used to illustrate the story of Jesus. Mark does not quote any of them, but reading between the lines of his Gospel, one constantly sees the rays of light that come forth from the suffering servant to illuminate the life of Jesus.

Opening Prayer

See, my servant shall prosper,
    he shall be raised high and greatly exalted.
Even as many were amazed at him—
    so marred was his look beyond that of man,
    and his appearance beyond that of mortals—
    ...

There was in him no stately bearing to make us
  look at him,
nor appearance that would attract us to him.
He was spurned and avoided by men,
  a man of suffering, accustomed to infirmity,
One of those from whom men hide their faces,
  spurned, and we held him in no esteem.

Yet it was our infirmities that he bore,
  our sufferings that he endured,
While we thought of him as stricken,
  as one smitten by God and afflicted.
But he was pierced for our offenses,
  crushed for our sins,
Upon him was the chastisement that makes us whole,
  by his stripes we were healed.[3]

RETREAT SESSION SIX

Mark continues:

For a whole generation (forty years), it never occurred
to us in the early Church that there would be any such
thing as a written gospel. We were quite content to gather
for the breaking of the bread. Over and over again, we
told the life-giving story of Jesus' Passion, death and
Resurrection. Also, we remembered and shared the words
of the apostles and other witnesses about how to live out
our lives with Jesus.

It was only with the tragic deaths of Peter and Paul,
with incredible torture and suffering, that my community
confronted me with the need for a written gospel. At each
gathering, we recounted the stories of the suffering of
Jesus. But what did his less than twenty-four-hour
experience of suffering have to do with our own?

The betrayal of Judas; the sleepy indifference of the disciples and the seizure by the soldiers in the garden; the trials before the high priest, the Sanhedrin and Pilate; the denial by Peter; the carrying of the cross and the crucifixion were all deeply moving stories. They were especially touching when told in the context of a loving, supportive community that gathered in peace for the breaking of the bread.

But then the atmosphere changed. Some of our members were being harassed, ridiculed and mocked in the synagogues for their belief in this "Christ." Nero, who had viciously ripped our leadership away from us, started in with the unimaginable torture of some of our number. They were covered with pitch and used as torches to illuminate his orgies. The fire that destroyed much of the city was blamed on us. Even the Roman Senate was disgusted with Nero and decreed his death. With the aid of a servant, he took a knife to his own throat and beat the senate to the punch. He was so evil that many were disappointed that they were not able to witness his funeral. That event was conducted under mysterious circumstances, giving rise to the rumor of *Nero Redivivus*, that Nero would come back to life.

You would have thought that we would have breathed a sigh of relief at Nero's passing, but we held our breath to see what would happen next. Things got worse. The next four Caesars all died violent deaths in less than a year. That created such a climate of fear and suspicion that every knock on the door was perceived as a threat. Vespasian was elected emperor by his troops in Palestine, and he left his son Titus there to put down the Jewish revolt and destroy my hometown, Jerusalem. Day after day, we heard nothing but bad news.

Some of us lost our lives, some fell into apostasy, and all were left with serious questions about where the Good

News fit in with all this tragedy. I wasn't quite sure that I had all the answers, but I did know that part of the problem was that people were asking the wrong questions.

"What did we do to deserve this?" That question springs from an inability to let go of an antiquated, immature and bankrupt spirituality. It is based upon what has been called "ambush theology," in which God is lurking out there just waiting for us to make a false move so he can punish us for breaking a law. Then he can revel in our discomfort.

I was raised on that kind of thinking. It was drummed into our minds from the end of the Book of Deuteronomy. It lists all of the blessings you will have for obeying the law and all of the curses that will befall you for breaking it. I can look back and smile about it now, but it scared me to death back then. Listen:

> But if you do not hearken to the voice of the LORD, your God, and are not careful to observe all his commandments...[t]he LORD will put a curse on you, defeat and frustration in every enterprise you undertake.... The LORD will strike you with Egyptian boils and with tumors, eczema and the itch....[and] with madness, blindness and panic.... Your ass will be stolen....[4]

Now that is enough to make you behave out of fear, but it just does not explain all the suffering that my community was experiencing. We had done no wrong that would have angered God. On the contrary, we had become disciples of his Son.

Others, knowing that God could not be held responsible for the present disasters, nor could we be blamed for them, posed a different question. Is not this evil that has come upon us the work of the Evil One? If our disasters could not be laid at the feet of God, then there must be a Satan, devil or Beelzebul who has the upper hand. And there's the rub: If Satan is in charge, then "Kingdom of God" would make a nice title for a book of fairy tales.

And Jesus is not lord. His enemies had sought to deprive him of his Lordship by making him a junior partner in the firm of Beelzebul and Sons.[5]

I have no illusions about the power of Satan. He exists, but he is not Lord. He may initiate a little skirmish here and there, but he has lost the war. Jesus is Lord!

And that leads to another question. If Jesus is risen as he said and if he's Lord of life and death, then why doesn't he do something about this mess? The disciples in Rome were beginning to feel like the disciples in the storm on the Sea of Galilee: "Teacher, do you not care that we are perishing?" That is probably more accurately made into this prayer: "Jesus Christ, don't you give a damn about what's happening?"[6] And as with his first disciples, his answer is: "Why are you terrified? Do you not have faith?" (But he does calm the storm, in his own time!)

Jesus did not provide any answers to the whys and wherefores of evil and suffering. He simply became one of us. Even while I was writing, a group arose in the Church who were called Docetists. Their belief was a marriage of Christianity and a dualism that despised the flesh. They bought into Plato's dictum that the soul was the prisoner of the body. The worst of it was that they considered it an insult to God to proclaim that his Son had become human. For them, Jesus was not really a human being, and his flesh was a phantasm, a chimera. They didn't like their own bodies, so they would not blaspheme God by believing that he took such an evil thing as a human body upon himself.

Not so! And I had to emphasize that in my Gospel.

Those who knew Jesus insisted that he was completely, totally, and without any reservation, like us. Those who were looking for a superhuman, without spot or wrinkle, rejected him precisely because he was too much like themselves. All the stories about him that came down to me from the community also insisted on his humanity being exactly like our own. He did not have a Teflon personality that was unaffected by our pain and anguish. His suffering did not start at noon on Good Friday.

As I began gathering and organizing the stories about him that had come down to me, it became evident that I would not be able to write two paragraphs about him without one of them telling of his suffering. Immediately after his Baptism and temptations, I had to let the reader know that John had been arrested. That must have hurt Jesus tremendously. If this was how the Baptist ended up, what could be in store for Jesus himself?

Jesus needed to pray. He could not face such an ominous future alone. Yet the crowds were consuming him. He had to deprive himself of sleep to be apart with his Father. His quiet was disturbed by his own disciples, and he was driven to go to those who had not yet heard his message of the Kingdom.

> The whole town was gathered at the door. He cured many who were sick with various diseases, and he drove out many demons, not permitting them to speak because they knew him. Rising very early before dawn, he left and went off to a deserted place, where he prayed. Simon and those who were with him, pursued him and on finding him said: "Everyone is looking for you." He told them, "Let us go to the nearby villages that I may preach there also. For this purpose have I come."[7]

Talk about suffering! I was exhausted, and I hadn't even finished the first chapter of my Gospel.

Then the trouble really started. The scribes, recognized as the professional theologians of the community, accused Jesus of blasphemy. That was not easy to take. While doing good, he was accused of the worst evil. And once they got started, they were like puppies with a bone. They publicly questioned his integrity and spirituality because of the "low class" of those he invited to discipleship.[8]

The litany continues. "Why don't he and his disciples fast?"[9] "Why do his disciples do what is unlawful on the sabbath?"[10] "Why does he cure on the sabbath?" Jesus had had it! He looked around at them with anger and grieved at their hardness of heart.[11]

Then, before I could even get out of Chapter Three, I had to tell how his relatives arrived on the scene, but not, as might be expected, to show that they were proud of him. "[T]hey set out to seize him, for they said, 'He is out of his mind.'" Then, in desperation, the "theologians" accused him of being in league with the devil.[12] I had not even finished writing one-fourth of the Gospel, and I was overwhelmed by the thought of the suffering that bombarded Jesus from every side. And I had not even touched upon the obtuseness, blind ambition and disloyalty of those whom he had chosen to support him and continue his work.

The cross was always clear on the horizon. Calvary was to be the summit of his sufferings, but not the total of them. It was not a surprise and tragic ending but the culmination of a life in which the shadow of the cross loomed ominously each day.

One of the stories about him that came down to me vividly expressed the suffering and frustration that were his daily fare. But, I really had to wrestle with the passage before I could make any sense of it. One time he quoted the words of Isaiah, as descriptive of his own ministry and his reason for teaching in parables. It was so that:

[T]hey may look and see but not perceive,
and hear and listen but not understand,
in order that they may not be converted
and be forgiven.[13]

This seems to contradict the very meaning of the vocation of a prophet, whether that prophet be Isaiah or Jesus. A prophet's role was to get people to perceive, understand and be forgiven. Indeed, Jesus had said that he spoke his word in parables precisely that his message might be understood.[14]

The only explanation for his identifying with the lament of Isaiah is the profound disappointment and frustration that they both felt toward the end of their lives at what was almost a total lack of response to their call and message. Those to whom they had been sent had not perceived, understood or sought forgiveness. Their obtuse stubbornness and hardness of heart seemed so incredible that it seemed to them to have been caused by something that was beyond human power.

But all of these sufferings and many more that are part of the gospel were not something that "happened" to Jesus. They became part of the gospel because they are part of the human condition. They are not unforeseen tragedies in which Jesus was the actor, and someone else was writing the scenario. They came upon Jesus because he embraced our humanity completely.

To the eye without faith, it looked like bad news. It was tragic. But for those who could see with the eyes of faith, his life was transformed from tragedy into redeeming sacrifice by one key element. One of the scribes, usually his implacable foes, tries to trap him, but unwittingly gives us the key to the problem of suffering. His answer to the scribe is neither legal disputation nor pedantic instruction. It is the story of his life. "'Hear, O Israel! The Lord our God is Lord alone! You shall love the

Lord your God with all your heart, with all your soul, with all your mind, and with all your strength.' The second is this: 'You shall love your neighbor as yourself.'"[15]

Jesus never said that he came to take away suffering. To do that, he would have had to take away our humanity. He came to show us that suffering need not be dehumanizing and diminishing. In writing the Gospel, I had to show my tortured and suffering fellow disciples in Rome that it was up to them to transform bad news into good news. They alone could do it, but they could not do it alone. They didn't have to. Jesus had been there before them and was with them now. So what do you do, instead of feeling sorry for yourself or being paralyzed by fear? "[T]hey went forth and preached everywhere, while the Lord worked with them and confirmed the word through accompanying signs."[16]

For Reflection

- Mark's friend Paul wrote to the Philippians and shared a vivid meditation on the self-emptying (Greek: *kenosis*) and exaltation of Jesus. But the line that introduces it is too often missed, and it is key. "Have among yourselves the same attitude that Christ Jesus had." Or, as I would translate it, "You ought to approach life with the same mind-set that Jesus Christ did." And to continue: "Who though he was really God, did not think his divine attributes something to be miserly about. No, he really let go, and, identifying with the dregs of humanity, he was indistinguishable from us, for the simple reason that he actually was one of us."[17] And that is the mind-set that Paul urges us all to have: to embrace our wounded, vulnerable

humanity with all its spots and wrinkles. The Son of
God did.

*How might my own mind-set be in better accord with that
of Jesus? What am I willing to do about this need for
change?*

■ *No religious philosophy or religious system has ever been
able to explain the problem of suffering. The simple
solutions of the offended God demanding justice or the
machinations of a Satan with horns and trident, remain
simplistic and condescending.*

> *It is valid to ask, "How can a good God permit the
senseless and chaotic evil that frequently seems about to
smother this creation?"*

> *The existentialist philosophers, confronted with the
brutal carnage of World War II, answered it by denying
God's existence. Their experience of evil was so
overpowering that they could not conceive of the existence
of a good God.*

> *Jesus avoids the simple answers that he learned in the
Hebrew Scriptures. He knew that the cry of Job is still
heard. But he also knew when confronted with the
simplistic question of his disciples: "[W]ho sinned, this man
or his parents ...?"[18] that God was still in charge, and even
suffering and evil could manifest his power. As Jesus' own
suffering shows, love is the key.*

> *What is my own response to the question of suffering?
For me, how is love the key?*

Closing Prayer

Read these inspired words of Saint Paul:

Love is patient, love is kind. It is not jealous, [love] is

not pompous, it is not inflated, it is not rude, it does not seek its own interests, it is not quick-tempered, it does not brood over injury, it does not rejoice over wrongdoing but rejoices with the truth. It bears all things, believes all things, hopes all things, endures all things.[19]

Try substituting your name for the word *love* and *he* or *she* for *it* in this passage. Then pray for help!

Notes

[1] Mark 13:32.

[2] Mark 10:30.

[3] Isaiah 52:13-15; 53:2b-5. Only a few verses are quoted here. It would be good to read Isaiah 52:13-53:12.

[4] Deuteronomy 28:15 *passim*.

[5] Mark 3:22ff.

[6] Mark 4:35ff.

[7] Mark 1:33-38.

[8] Mark 2:14-16.

[9] Mark 2:18.

[10] Mark 2:24.

[11] Mark 3:5.

[12] Mark 3:21ff.

[13] Mark 4:12.

[14] Mark 4:33.

[15] Mark 12:29b-31a.

[16] Mark 16:20.

[17] Philippians 2:5ff (author's translation.)

[18] John 9:2.

[19] 1 Corinthians 13.

DAY SEVEN
Jesus: The Cornerstone Rejected

Coming Together in the Spirit

Most people I know would not include among their major accomplishments the amount of time they had spent suffering. Our standards usually gauge the worth of a person by real estate, bank account or jewelry. "Diamonds are a girl's best friend" contains more truth than humor. In some of the more notorious recent trials, the lawyers' time was worth from $200 to $500 an hour. And when damages were awarded, the jury decided how much the loss of a person's presence was worth.

Suffering, however, is not listed among the assets. It goes right to the debit column. It is seen as a curse and an evil. Paul, the theologian, when he was a rabbi, perceived suffering as did all the other rabbis, as the righteous punishment of a vindictive God.

But when he met Jesus, he saw things differently. "For his sake I have accepted the loss of all things and I consider them so much rubbish, that I may gain Christ, and be found in him, not having any righteousness of my own based on the law but that which comes through faith in Christ, the righteousness from God, depending on faith to know him and the power of his resurrection and the

71

sharing of his sufferings by being conformed to his death...."[1]

Defining Our Thematic Context

In the Byzantine period an emperor issued an edict forbidding the cross to be included in floor designs in churches, lest it be walked on.

In the Eastern churches one of the major feasts is the Exultation of the Holy Cross. That is how Jesus saw the cross. It is a symbol not of death but of life, not of defeat but of triumph. Love is the difference.

When Jesus invites, "Come, follow me," he beckons to the glory that he prefigured on Tabor. But that cannot be reached without the cross. There are no shortcuts to it. We cannot detour around Good Friday to get to Easter Sunday.

Opening Prayer

We adore you most Holy Lord, Jesus Christ, and we bless you, because by your holy cross you have redeemed the World.—*Francis of Assisi*

RETREAT SESSION SEVEN

Mark continues:

In our day, we had plenty of couches, but we reclined on them to eat, not to have our psyches probed by a psychiatrist. So the questions that people ask today did not occur to us. When did Jesus know that he was God? When was he aware of his role as messiah? When did he perceive that the apparent tragedy of the cross would be eclipsed by the resurrection? All we knew is that he was totally possessed by the desire to do the will of his Father. He was a driven man, and he was not an unwilling actor in the drama that unfolded.

He revealed his insights as a theologian with his masterful reinterpretation of the vineyard story of Isaiah.[2] He made it autobiographical, putting himself in the picture as the son of the owner of the vineyard. But Jesus makes a major twist in the story. In Isaiah, the owner's plans for the vineyard are frustrated. There is no crop worth harvesting. So the vineyard is allowed to revert to a wasteland. But in Jesus' variation on the theme, the heir is murdered by the avaricious and jealous tenants. It is they who are punished, not the vineyard.

Then, mixing the metaphor, Jesus switches from horticulture to architecture: "Have you not read this scripture passage:

> 'The stone that the builders rejected
>   has become the cornerstone;
> by the Lord has this been done,
>   and it is wonderful in our eyes'?"[3]

The insult is obvious. Either they, the "biblical scholars," have not read the Scriptures, or they have missed this particular text. Why? Because they were experts on the texts where they thought the messiah's job description was to be found, and they decided that this was not one of them. They had God and his ways all figured out. In their religion, there was no room for the God of surprises. However, their next move is no surprise: "They were seeking to arrest him, but they feared the crowd, for they realized that he had addressed the parable to them."[4]

The "builders" are at work, but their rejection is not unexpected. He had hardly ever said a word or performed a sign that was not the object of their scrutiny, cynical criticism and dismissal. Not only had they missed what Jesus quoted from the psalms but they had also missed a prophetic text that should have been the foundation of their spirituality.

> Seek the LORD while he may be found,
>   call him while he is near....
> For my thoughts are not your thoughts,
>   nor are your ways my ways, says the LORD.
> As high as the heavens are above the earth,
>   so high are my ways above your ways
>   and my thoughts above your thoughts.[5]

They should have learned from the great prophet Elijah, that sometimes God does not act as if he is going for an Academy Award.

We also have to be ready to hear him in "the still small voice" or more accurately, the voice of "a tiny whispering sound."[6]

I would have loved to have given a favorable progress report on Jesus' first disciples, but that was not the information that was handed on to me. "They had not understood the incident of the loaves. On the contrary, their hearts were hardened."[7] I'm sorry if it sounds trite, but the thought must have crossed Jesus' mind, "With friends like these, who needs enemies?" His patience was wearing thin. "Do you not yet understand or comprehend? Are your hearts hardened? Do you have eyes and not see, ears and not hear?"[8]

From our privileged positions bolstered by the perspectives of time and resurrection faith, it is all too easy to cast judgments on Jesus' friends as well as his enemies. "If we had been there, etc., etc., etc." Better we should take to heart:

> Whoever wishes to come after me must deny himself, take up his cross, and follow me. For whoever wishes to save his life will lose it, but whoever loses his life for my sake and that of the gospel will save it. What profit is there for one to gain the whole world and forfeit his life? What could one give in exchange for his life? Whoever is ashamed of me and of my words in this faithless and sinful generation, the Son of Man will be ashamed of when he comes in his Father's glory with the holy angels.[9]

Looking back from almost forty years later, as I was writing the Gospel, I had to remind myself constantly that there was only one reason why I first picked up a pen. It was to repeat over and over the invitation of Jesus, "Come, follow me." But, unwittingly I had bought into the standards and values of the people around me. The Romans were always aping the Greeks, and philosophy was all the rage. I had tried to explain the logic of the cross and the consequential finality of the Resurrection. They laughed! I should have, too. I was trying to pour new wine into old wineskins and wasn't even aware of it.

I made myself look even more ludicrous when I tried to show the Jews that based upon the obvious workings of God in their history, the cross was the natural manifestation of his greatness. I only provoked their anger. "How dare you compare the mighty acts of God—by which he had brought about creation, and triumphantly led our people from slavery to freedom, to be a people all his own—with the cross of a criminal?" They tripped over that. God just did not function that way.

Checking around, I found that I was in good company. Paul had run into the same problem in evangelizing the Corinthians. Both he and I had tried to promote the cross with all the eloquence and persuasion we could muster, but we were not heard.

> The message of the cross is foolishness to those who are perishing, but to us who are being saved it is the power of God. For it is written:
> "I will destroy the wisdom of the wise, and the learning of the learned I will set aside."
> Where is the wise one? Where is the scribe? Where is the debater of this age? Has not God made the wisdom of the world foolish? For since in the wisdom of God, the world did not come to know God through wisdom, it was the will of God through the foolishness of the proclamation to save those who have faith. For Jews demand signs and Greeks look for wisdom, but we proclaim Christ crucified, a stumbling block to Jews and foolishness to Gentiles, but to those who are called, Jews and Greeks alike, Christ the power of God and the wisdom of God.[10]

I had checked notes with Paul, and we both came to the same conclusion: There is no logic to the cross. I should have suspected that. Three times Jesus predicted that it was in his future.[11] He did not explain it. He did not apologize for it. He gave not the slightest hint that there was a way to get around it. He just dropped it into our arms.

Zebedee's unselfish genes must have run out, because, after Jesus' third prediction of the cross, his sons asked the most selfish, unfeeling question I ever heard. "Jesus, when you become CEO, would you make sure that we are in line for top executive positions?" Naturally, the other ten were put out, but not because the brothers had been so ambitious. The others were disturbed that James and John had gotten to Jesus first.

Obviously, three predictions of the cross and Resurrection did not impress that crowd. Jesus should have walked away and thrown up his arms in disgust. I would have. But "'my thoughts are not your thoughts, nor are your ways my ways,' says the LORD."[12] So Jesus tried a different tack. "You know that those who are recognized as rulers over the Gentiles lord it over them, and their great ones make their authority over them felt. But it shall not be so among you. Rather, whoever wishes to be great among you will be your servant; whoever wishes to be first among you will be the slave of all."[13]

The God of surprises is at it again. That's not the way things are supposed to work. Whatever happened to "rank has its privileges"?

When I was editing the text of my Gospel, I put the story of Jesus' cure of the blind Bartimaeus right after this stupid skirmish of the disciples, because it ends with: "Jesus told him, 'Go your way, your faith has saved you.' Immediately he received his sight and followed him on the way."[14] I thought it was important at this point to have at least one disciple with a little faith and some vision!

But I'm jumping ahead of the story. Jesus concludes the account of the ambition and "fraternal correction" of his disciples with one of his most important utterances. (The so-called "Jesus Seminar" may have reservations about its authenticity, but Peter had no doubt about it, nor do I!) He said: "For the Son of Man did not come to be served but to serve and to give his life as a ransom for many."[15]

With this statement, Jesus identifies himself with a

whole category of people in the Hebrew Scriptures: the redeemers. It is the title given to the person who is related to one who lacks *shalom*, and is therefore obligated to restore it to them. Shalom means not just peace, but fullness of life, the possibility of living up to the promise that is within you, in a word, completeness. The lack of shalom may be the result of dying without offspring, and thus being deprived of immortality. That's what the claims of Tamar on Juda[16] and his sons, her deceased husband's brothers, and Ruth on Boaz[17] are all about.

The claim on the nearest relative may arise from any deprivation of shalom: slavery, loss of hereditary property, being orphaned or widowed, etc. The one who restored shalom was the "redeemer." It is no surprise that it became one of Israel's favorite titles for their God. He had proven that he was their redeemer when he ransomed them from the oppression of Pharaoh: "You have seen for yourselves how I treated the Egyptians and how I bore you up on eagle wings, and brought you here to myself."[18] Thereafter, at any time when their shalom was threatened, Israel knew where to turn. Lord,

> Come and ransom my life;
> as an answer for my enemies, redeem me.[19]

It was in the desperate situation of the Babylonian exile that a prophet[20] gives hope to a people who thought they had been abandoned by their God.

> But now, thus says the LORD,
> who created you, O Jacob, and formed you, O Israel:
> Fear not, for I have redeemed you;
> I have called you by name: you are mine.[21]

And lest it be forgotten that the obligation of redemption falls on the closest relative:

> Fear not, you shall not be put to shame;

you need not blush, for you shall not be disgraced.
The shame of your youth you shall forget,
    the reproach of your widowhood no longer remember.
For he who has become your husband is your Maker;
    his name is the LORD of hosts;
Your redeemer is the Holy One of Israel,
    called God of all the earth.

The LORD calls you back,
    like a wife forsaken and grieved in spirit,
A wife married in youth and then cast off,
    says your God.
For a brief moment I abandoned you,
    but with great tenderness I will take you back.
In an outburst of wrath, for a moment
    I hid my face from you;
But with enduring love I take pity on you,
    says the LORD, your redeemer.[22]

It is into this whole context of redemption that Jesus places his cross. It is the way by which he will be our ransom. What God did for the exiles, Jesus does for us. He restores us to shalom. And we should not miss the reality that he becomes our redeemer precisely because it is the obligation of the nearest relative. He is our brother, and therefore, our redeemer.

For Reflection

- *When Saint Francis of Assisi knelt before the crucifix in the church of San Damiano, he saw a cross with the figure of a youthful, vibrant, alert Jesus, surrounded by his disciples. Later generations showed him dead and lifeless, as if conquered by the cross. How does my own spirituality reflect the vibrant Jesus who drew Francis into discipleship?*

- *The message of Paul in 1 Corinthians 1:18 is paraphrased in the hymn:*

Lift high the cross, the love of Christ proclaim,
til all the world adore his Sacred Name.

Led on their way by this triumphant sign
the hosts of God, in conquering ranks combine.

O Lord once lifted on the glorious tree,
as thou hast promised, draw the world to thee.

*Sing this or any other triumphant hymn that stirs the fire of
your love for Christ.*

- *In Handel's* Messiah, *the Hallelujah Chorus on the triumph
of Christ is immediately followed by the aria from Job,
concluded by Paul's words in 1 Corinthians 15:20. If you can,
listen to it with Saint Mark:*

I know that my Redeemer liveth,
and he shall stand at the latter day upon the earth.
And tho' worms destroy this body,
yet in my flesh I shall see God.
For now is Christ risen from the dead,
the first fruits of them that sleep.

*How does the experience of reflecting on this powerful music
affect you?*

- Job's wrestling with the mystery of suffering provides
insight for the wrestling that the disciple must do with
the mystery of the cross. In his revision of R.A.F.
MacKenzie's commentary on the Book of Job, Roland
Murphy sheds helpful light.[23]

  The author makes the three friends...eloquent
defenders of the "traditional" view of divine
retribution.... The writer's purpose is not to ridicule the
traditional doctrine, but to show that it is simply
inadequate. Insofar as this doctrine is positive, it is
sound and helpful (cf. Psalm 37, simple to the point of

naïveté, yet beautiful and consoling). It contains much moral and religious truth but they spoil it by exaggeration. They are not willing to leave a margin of uncertainty, to admit limits to their understanding, to write after each of their theses "If God so wills." All the workings of divine providence must be clear to them, explicit, mathematical. They have fallen victims to the occupational hazard of theologians: they forget they are dealing with mystery. They have "studied" God as a subject to be analyzed, predicted, and understood. And in forcing facts to agree with their understanding, they become willfully dishonest. (Job 13:6-11) Meantime, the reader of the book knows what the friends (and Job) do not know.[24]

What insights into suffering have you gained from experience, prayer and the willingness to trust in Jesus?

Closing Prayer

May the God of peace, who brought up from the dead the great shepherd of the sheep by the blood of the eternal covenant, Jesus our Lord, furnish you with all that is good, that you may do his will. May he carry out in you what is pleasing to him through Jesus Christ, to whom be glory forever [and ever]. Amen.[25]

Notes

1 Philippians 3:8b-10ff.
2 Isaiah 5 = Mark 12.
3 Mark 12:10-11.
4 Mark 12:12.
5 Isaiah 55:6; 8-9.
6 1 Kings 19:12b.
7 Mark 6:52.
8 Mark 8:17-18.
9 Mark 8:34b-38.
10 1 Corinthians 1:18-25.
11 See Mark 8:31; 9:31; 10:34.
12 Cf. note 5 above.
13 Mark 10:42-44.
14 Mark 10:52.
15 Mark 10:45.
16 See Genesis 38.
17 See Ruth 4:5.
18 Exodus 19:4.
19 Psalm 69:19.
20 Isaiah 40—55.
21 Isaiah 43:1.
22 Isaiah 54:4-8.
23 "Lift High the Cross," copyright © 1974, Hope Publishing Co.
24 R.A.F. MacKenzie, S.J., and Roland E. Murphy, O.Carm., "Job," in *New Jerome Biblical Commentary*, Raymond Brown, S.S., Joseph Fitzmyer, S.J., and Roland Murphy, O.Carm., eds. (Englewood Cliffs, N.J.: Prentice-Hall, 1990), p. 467.
25 Hebrews 13:20.

Going Forth to Live the Theme

St. John Lateran in Rome, and not St. Peter's in the Vatican, is the pope's cathedral. In the piazza across the street from St. John Lateran is a heroic statue of Saint Francis of Assisi. If you stand behind the statue with its outstretched arms, you will see the illusion of Francis holding up and supporting the "head and mother of all churches." The sculpture commemorates the visit of the Poverello to Innocent III in 1210.

He came with his small band of followers seeking approbation of their way of life. Innocent III, one of the greatest popes since Saint Peter, was obsessed by the Humiliati, Cathari and other reform movements that condemned the Church as an obstacle to the Christian life. The little man from Assisi and his followers, kneeling before Innocent, looked suspiciously like all the other rag-tag enthusiasts who had come down the Appian Way. One thing was different: They came not to condemn and criticize the pope but to beg his support and approval.

Innocent III was a renowned canon lawyer. He asks what rule the brothers will follow. When Francis replied, "The Holy Gospel," the pope knew that he had an impractical band of idealists and dreamers on his hands. According to legend, Innocent withheld approval and sought a good night's sleep. But that sleep was disturbed by a dream of a little man holding up the collapsing Lateran Basilica. Dawn found Innocent's approval forthcoming, and thus was born the order whose rule is

"to observe the Holy Gospel of Our Lord Jesus Christ."
Living the gospel may be difficult, but it is not the
"impossible dream." By doing it, Francis had a profound
effect on history and the Church. Through his gospel life
and spirituality, he brought about a profound renewal. At
the beginning of his council, John XXIII went as a pilgrim
to Assisi begging Francis' assistance in the *aggiornamento*.

In this age after Vatican II, the Church still needs those
who will revivify and renew her. Anyone can do a retread
of the institution and the structures. It takes saints who are
serious about the power of the gospel and who embrace it
with unreserved love to evangelize and transform this
Church into a credible sign of the Body of Christ for the
third millennium.

Mark was the first to convey Jesus' invitation at the
beginning of the first millennium. The invitation still
stands and still has an R.S.V.P. attached.

Deepening Your Acquaintance

Books

Instruction on the Historicity of the Gospels. This decree by
the Pontifical Biblical Commission with the approval of
Paul VI emerged from a vicious behind-the-scenes
struggle at Vatican II. Catholic biblical scholars were
being accused of heresy or worse, and the biblical
movement was almost set back fifty years. The
instruction is now the official teaching of the Church on
how to understand the threefold formation of the
Gospels. Vatican Press, 1964.

Understanding the New Testament by Stephen C. Doyle,
O.F.M. (the author of this retreat book), is a popular and
attractive introduction to all the books of the New
Testament. It contains a synopsis and explanation of the
above mentioned instruction. St. Anthony Messenger
Press and Franciscan Communications, 1988.

Commentaries

Daniel J. Harrington, S.J., has done a fine one for the *New
Jerome Biblical Commentary* (Prentice-Hall, 1990). In
addition to the original insights of the author, it is a
good compendium of the best of contemporary Markan
scholarship. Much the same in a bit more popular and
pastoral vein and with some splendid insights is done

by Pheme Perkins for the *New Interpreters Bible*, Vol. VIII
(Abingdon, 1995). Both of them contain rich lodes of
bibliographical resources.

Kurtz, Ernest, and Katherine Ketcham. *The Spirituality of
Imperfection* (paperback). New York: Bantam Books,
1994.

Videos

Jesus: Who Do Men Say That I Am? Responses to the
question from ordinary people and biblical scholars.
Available from Videos With Values, 1-800-233-4629.

Messiah, George Frederic Handel. Performed by London
Baroque Players and Cardiff Polyphonic Choir.
Available from Gateway Films/Vision Media,
1-800-523-0226.

*Seeking Jesus in His Own Land: A Scriptural Pilgrimage With
Fr. Stephen Doyle, O.F.M.* St. Anthony Messenger Press
and Franciscan Communications, 1-800-488-0488.

St. Mark's Gospel. A one-man presentation by Alec
McGowen. Available from Palisades Home Video,
1-800-989-8576.

Yeshua: The Promise, the Land, the Messiah. Jesus interpreted
through ancient Jewish beliefs. Available from
Wellspring Media, 1-800-538-5856.